DEVOTIONS TO MAKE YOU STRONGER

OTHER BOOKS IN THE GROWING 2:52 LIBRARY

2:52 Boys Bible

2:52 NIV Backpack Bible

2:52 Creepy Creatures & Bizarre Beasts from the Bible

2:52 Bible Heroes & Bad Guys

2:52 Bible Angels & Demons

2:52 Big, Bad Bible Giants

2:52 Bible Wars & Weapons

2:52 Weird & Gross Bible Stuff

2:52 How to Draw Big, Bad Bible Beasts

2:52 How to Draw Big, Bad, and Ugly Bible Guys

DEVOTIONS TO MAKE YOU Stronger

ED STRAUSS

zonderkidz

ZONDERVAN.com/
AUTHORTRACKER
follow your favorite authors

The children's group of Zondervan

www.zonderkidz.com

2:52/Devotions to Make You Stronger

Requests for information should be addressed to:
Zonderkidz, Grand Rapids, Michigan 49530

Library of Congress Cataloging-in-Publication Data

Strauss, Ed, 1953-
Devotions to make you stronger : a 90-day devotional / by Ed Strauss.
p. cm. -- (2:52 library)
ISBN-13: 978-0-310-71311-1 (softcover)
ISBN-10: 0-310-71311-0 (softcover)
1. Boys--Prayer-books and devotions--English. I. Title.
BV4855.S77 2007
242'.62--dc22

2006023521

Editor: Barbara Scott
Art direction and design: Merit Alderink
Interior compositon: Christine Orejuela-Winkelman

Printed in the United States of America

08 09 10 11 12 • 10 9 8 7 6 5 4 3

table of contents

devotion #1

MADE FOR ACTION

Moses was educated in all the wisdom of the Egyptians and was powerful in speech and action.

— Acts 7:22

One day Pharaoh's daughter went down to the Nile River and found this cute little Israelite kid floating in a basket, so she adopted him and called him Moses. He grew up as a royal prince — and Egyptian princes back then got a top education. So he was smart, but Moses was also strong. He loved *action*! He got out and *did* stuff! One of the favorite sports of Egyptian princes was hippopotamus hunting. Can't you just see Moses snatching a spear and jumping into the thick of it? Talk about *action* — foaming and bloody water, capsized boats, snapped spears, snapped legs. . .

Hmmm. . .maybe you'd better give hippo hunting a pass. Your local zoo probably has half a dozen rules against spearing hippos anyway. But there are other cool, active things you can do: white-water rafting (okay, maybe not *yet*), racing go-carts, wrestling, swimming, bicycling, or playing a game of soccer.

Boys' bodies are packed with energy. God designed you for action, so don't sit around all day playing computer games. Exercising your thumb does not count as a full-body workout. You may not be into sports — maybe you'd rather be watching TV. Fine. Get in your TV and computer time, but you *also* gotta get out and *move* it if you don't want to end up looking like a Jabba the Hutt.

Talk about action figures — God made you to *be* one. You need exercise! Have you had yours today?

devotion #2

KEEP IT FLOWING

When Samson drank, his strength returned and he revived.

—Judges 15:19

Even Samson the Strong lost his strength when he hadn't drunk water in a while. He'd just finished wasting one thousand Philistines, and then he staggered among the piles of corpses, muttering, "Must I now die of thirst?" (No one answered; they were all dead.) Fortunately, God showed him a water spring, and Samson lay on the ground and chugged the cool stuff down. You thought Samson's strength was only from his long hair? Hey, the guy had to *drink water* to keep his strength up too.

Most people today don't drink nearly enough water. If all you're getting is a glass of milk in the morning, a juice box at lunch, and a glass of water at dinner, you're not even halfway there! Your body can get dehydrated (dried out) — and then you're in trouble. You can get headaches, or worse.

Want to avoid grief? Drink six to eight glasses of liquid a day. Sure, you'll be peeing more, but God designed your urine to carry poisonous wastes out of your body. Drink too little water, and the golden stream nearly dries up. By the way, make most of your liquid intake *water*. Drink that much soda pop and you'll have a sugar buzz. They'll be peeling you off the ceiling.

The Bible does not say, "Thou shalt drink water," but common sense tells you that you need to keep your tank full.

Devotion #3

IN TRAINING

Everyone who competes in the games goes into strict training.

—1 Corinthians 9:25

The apostle Paul lived in the city of Corinth for two years, and after he left he wrote to the Christians there. Now, a funny thing, often when Paul explained spiritual things to them, he used the language of training for athletic competitions. Why? Because Corinthians were passionate sports fans. Corinthians not only trained for the Olympic Games every four years, they also hosted the Isthmian Games every *two* years. And the Christians there went wild in the stands like everybody else.

You still need to train for competitions today. Whether you're into basketball, hockey, or martial arts, it takes

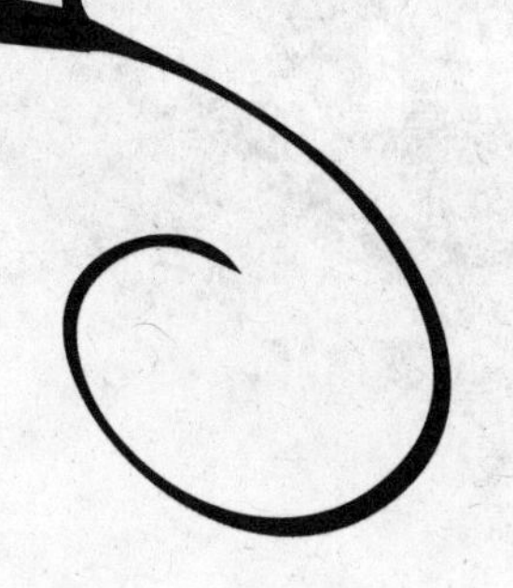

dedication and focus to become good at it. It helps if you absolutely *love* the sport, because all that repetition can get boring at times. You also have to know the game's rules. Like them or not, that's how the game is played, so your coach makes you learn them by heart and makes sure you follow them.

Today, just as in Paul's day, Christian life is like athletic training. You need to be as wild about Christ as the Corinthians were about their sports events. When you're passionate about something, it's easy to be devoted to it. And when you're devoted to something, you accept the repetitive training and strict rules as part of the package.

Stay passionate, stay focused, and all the rest will follow. That's true both in sports and in being a Christian.

Devotion #4

LOOKS AIN'T ALL

In all Israel there was not a man so highly praised for his handsome appearance as Absalom.

— 2 Samuel 14:25

King David was a very handsome guy, and he married Maacah, the drop-dead gorgeous princess of Geshur. Well, *no big surprise* that their son Absalom was so good-looking! From the top of his head to the end of his big toe, there wasn't a blemish on him. There wasn't even one freckle out of place. Problem was Absalom was in love with how he looked. He thought his hair was so cool, he let it grow down to his butt. He had five pounds of curly locks!

Absalom's outside might have been picture-perfect, but his heart was seriously messed up. This is the guy who killed his older brother, tried to murder his father, and raped ten women up on the palace roof where everyone could see them. Whoa! Talk about a mess! If you think that Absalom sounds like a Hollywood star with his life out of control, you got *that* one right! Some dudes don't make good role models no matter what kind of celebrity they are.

It's nice if you're good-looking, but that really isn't the important thing. If you don't know right from wrong, looks don't count for much. Are you ready for this one? The Bible says that a good-looking person with no morals is like a gold ring stuck through the snotty snout of a *pig*! (Proverbs 11:22)

You can be plain, or you can be a looker; it really doesn't matter. What's important is to have godly character.

devotion #5

UNMISTAKABLE SMELL

When Isaac caught the smell of his clothes, he blessed him and said, "Ah, the smell of my son is like the smell of a field."

— Genesis 27:27

Jacob wanted to have the oldest son blessing, but there was one little problem: Jacob's twin brother, Esau, was the oldest. That meant the blessing belonged to *him*. Jacob's mom, Rebekah, had a crooked plan. Since Isaac was blind, Jacob could go in, pretending to be Esau. So "Rebekah took the best clothes of Esau her older son, which she had in the house, and put them on her younger son Jacob" (Genesis 27:15).

Jacob walked into Dad's tent, and when Isaac got a whiff of those robes, he recognized Esau's *unmistakable smell* — and gave Jacob the blessing. See, Esau was a hunter. He crawled in the dirt, sneaking up on animals. No way his mom could get all the sweat stains and antelope poop out in the wash. But these were Esau's *best* clothes. What was he doing getting *these* clothes dirty and smelly?

And the *big* question: do you do the same thing? No, don't answer that. But when your mom says to change out of your good clothes, do it right away before you forget. Fold 'em, hang 'em up, or hurl 'em in the laundry — whatever it takes. If you crawl around in your best clothes, not even detergent will get out the dog poop smell.

Funny thing about Esau: he was *seventy-seven* years old, and he *still* hadn't clued in! Hey, but it's still not too late for you to start taking care of your clothing.

devotion #6

RUNNING OUT OF BOUNDS

If anyone competes as an athlete, he does not receive the victor's crown unless he competes according to the rules.

— 2 Timothy 2:5

The apostle Paul lived during Roman times, which was a great time to be living if you liked sports. The Romans were big into racing, boxing, wrestling, long jumping, discus throwing, javelin throwing, and chariot racing. Back then if you won an athletic competition, you got a crown of leaves. These days you get a colored ribbon. But even then every event had rules, and you had to compete according to those rules.

If your school has a track and field event, and some kid gets ahead by tripping his competition, think he's

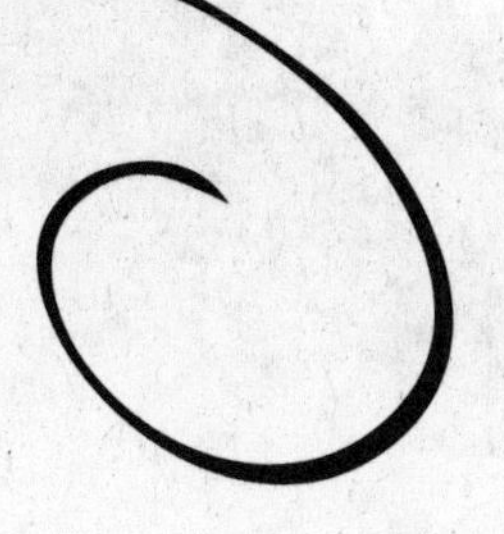

going to get a ribbon? Nope. He just disqualified himself. Also, cheating by cutting outside the lines may get you to the finish line first, but about three hundred spectators will be leaping out of their seats and howling, "Cheater!" Bodycheck some kid during a basketball game, and you're parking your sorry butt on the bench for a while.

Rules exist for good reasons, and if you don't obey them, all your skill and speed is of no use. You could be the best player on the team, but if you're sitting out a penalty, you'll only be playing with your shoelaces. It's the same with following God. His rules in the Bible aren't just to keep you from having fun. They exist to keep you and others safe.

You want the prize? Remember the rules and don't go running out of bounds.

Devotion #7

ALIEN FUNGI

"I have seen something that looks like mildew in my house."

— Leviticus 14:35

You know what mildew is? It's a whitish growth that sometimes appears on walls and ceilings inside houses. You sometimes see black mold moving in too. Mildews and molds were a problem in ancient Israel, and they're still a pain — especially if your room is warm and humid and you never open the window to air the place out. Your bedroom is private, right, but it shouldn't *smell* private.

Not only do mildew and mold look yucky, but they can cause health risks. If you have asthma, they can make you seriously ill. Even if you don't have asthma, they can sicken you. And mold growing on plates of half-eaten food under your bed? That stuff can be deadly. Sweaty, dirty socks can give you athlete's foot, and the itch can nearly drive you crazy. The list goes on and on.

If you see something strange, tell your parents. It could be alien fungus taking over the world, beginning with your bedroom (just kidding). Check stuff out, and you can solve problems before they even start. And while you're at it, take those dishes to the kitchen and dump your dirty jeans in the laundry. If your socks are grimy and slimy, change them.

If you get in the habit of taking care of details, good things will start happening, and bad things will stop happening. One thing for sure: at least the mildew and mold won't get you.

devotion #8

FULL-MEAL DEAL

"See how my eyes brightened when I tasted a little of this honey."

—1 Samuel 14:29

One day the Israelites were fighting the Philistines, and King Saul said something dumb like, "Nobody eats until the battle's won!" So here are the Israelites chasing the Phillies through the forest, but they're out of energy 'cause no one's eaten for hours. Suddenly they see honey oozing out of a bee's nest. No one goes for it except Prince Jonathan, and he immediately perks up. Jonathan's attitude was, "We'd do a better job fighting if we weren't famished out of our skulls."

Jonathan said, "See how my eyes brightened!" The moral? If you want shiny eyes, eat honey. That's why bears' eyes shine in the dark (just kidding). But the fact is, when you're beat, a snack can give you an energy boost and keep you going. In fact if you don't eat a good enough breakfast, your brain won't have the energy to work properly in school. Do that often enough and your grades will sink like the Titanic.

Your intestines break food down into natural sugars, and it's those sugars that drive your engine. That doesn't mean go for candy and chocolate though. Sure, they'll give you an energy jolt. . .then leave you flatter than you were before. Your body needs the full-meal deal. Shovel it *all* in: the potatoes, the beef, the carrots, and the fruit. Your intestines know what to do with that stuff even if you don't.

Want bright eyes and a bright brain? Eat your breakfast. Eat your lunch and dinner.

devotion #9

VIGOR MEANS POWER

"Of what use was the strength of their hands to me, since their vigor had gone from them?"

—Job 30:2

Job was a wealthy man, and besides everything else, he owned seven thousand sheep. He needed shepherds to protect them, otherwise wolves and lions would eat 'em, or raiders would ride in and rustle 'em. Taking care of sheep was hard work, and shepherds needed to be in shape to fight. Now, Job was always helping the poor, but he didn't give a job to just anybody. Some guys were so weak that Job couldn't even put them to work watching his sheep.

It's the same today. You may need to earn money, but no way an adult's gonna hire you if your vigor, or power, has gone from you. If you're so out of shape that you can't do the job, you'll miss out on fun activities and chances to earn money. You can't help it if you're smaller than other kids, but you *can* take care of the bod you have.

If you don't want vigor going out of you, you have to do three things: (1) eat good food so you can grow like you should to be at maximum strength; (2) get enough sleep, because you can't be strong if you're exhausted; and (3) exercise daily to stay fit. Follow these guidelines and you'll be in shape when a cash-earning job comes along.

Don't want to miss a fun outing? Stay healthy. Want to earn some extra cash? Stay strong.

devotion #10

LAST-MINUTE SCRAMBLE

A sluggard does not plow in season;
so at harvest time he looks
but finds nothing.
— Proverbs 20:4

The ground in Israel was usually so hard and dry that plows could barely break it up. But every September the rains softened the soil. That's when farmers were out with their oxen and plows, planting crops. Everyone except for sluggards, that is. Those lazy guys kept putting the job off. By the time they finally got around to it, the ground was getting hard again. They plowed and scattered seeds, sure, but come harvest (surprise, surprise!) no crop — or a very poor crop.

Sound familiar? Instead of doing your homework or school assignment when you're supposed to, do you put

it off till the last possible minute or only remember it at bedtime? If it's due the next day, do you do a rushed, sloppy job and get a low grade? This is called *procrastination*. A procrastinator knows what he's supposed to do but doesn't want to do it, so he drags his feet until it becomes an all-out emergency.

It's easy to avoid that last-minute scramble: do your homework when you're supposed to. Or if you're getting ready for school or church, stay focused on dressing, combing your hair, and finding your shoes. That way you can walk to the car instead of running there half-clothed and barefoot.

Don't be a sluggard. Roll up your sleeves and do your work when it's supposed to be done. Get it done and out of the way. Then go have your fun.

Devotion #11

GROW LIKE A STATUE?

And the boy Samuel continued to grow in stature.

—1 Samuel 2:26

Samuel didn't grow like a statue; he grew in *stature* — which means taller and bigger with strong bones and tough meat wrapped around his bones. When Samuel was just a little guy, his mom dropped him off with the high priest in Shiloh. That's where Samuel grew from a boy into a teen and then a young man.

Like Samuel, all kids grow. When you're about ten, you start going through a stage called puberty, and later you begin growing like crazy! This is called a *growth spurt*. By the time you hit fourteen or so, you're shooting up about four inches a year and starting to get some serious muscles. Now, you may be wondering, "How come *my* transformation hasn't kicked in yet?" Don't sweat it. It hits some boys earlier and other boys later.

Of course, your body *can't* grow tall and muscular all by itself. You have to throw fuel in your engine by eating properly and getting sleep. You've heard that smoking will stunt your growth, right? Well, a steady diet of junk food is *also* a bad stunt. So avoid guzzling down too much soda pop or wolfing down too many french fries, chips, and candy. Otherwise you'll get fatter and unhealthier when you should be getting taller and stronger.

Want to grow? Go for healthy food — meat, starches, fruit, and veggies. You need all of that stuff even if your taste buds try to lie to you and say that you don't.

devotion #12

BE HAPPY, YOUNG MAN

Be happy, young man, while you are young, and let your heart give you joy in the days of your youth.

— Ecclesiastes 11:9

Here's a command kids gotta love: Thou shalt have fun! It isn't exactly a commandment, but it's great advice. Now, King Solomon wasn't saying, "Goof off and play all day." Kids played back then, but they *also* did chores. And he wasn't saying, "Enjoy yourself now, 'cause it's only work when you get older." It's in the attitude. Anybody at any age can enjoy life. Like Solomon said, "However many years a man may live, let him enjoy them all" (verse 8).

Kids are hardwired to want to have fun, and as long as your home-

work and chores are done, go for it! We all need to unwind after a hard day. But it helps to have a positive attitude about school, homework, and chores too. If you complain about them, it'll seem like it takes *forever* to get through them. Hey, things really aren't so bad. You're not shoveling chicken dung all day long.

Whatever the chore, plant the thought in your mind, "I *have* to do this so I might as well have a good attitude." Even if you don't enjoy it, you can whistle while you work. Well, not out loud during a math test, but in other words, have a positive attitude. It beats *whining* while you work.

Put your heart into your work and try to enjoy it. It'll make things go faster. Then you'll be done sooner and can have some *real* fun.

Devotion #13

BE CONSIDERATE OF ROSES

"He must wash his clothes and bathe himself with fresh water, and he will be clean."

— Leviticus 15:13

When God gave Moses this law, the Israelites had just spent 430 years in Egypt. Now that they were leaving the pagan Egyptian culture behind, God wanted to make sure they didn't stop the *good* stuff — like washing. See, the ancient Egyptians were clean freaks. A historian named Herodotus wrote that the Egyptians would rather be clean than good-looking. They were very careful to always wear newly washed linen. The Egyptians bathed in the canals every morning and used soap. They even had mouthwash.

It was hard for the Israelites to stay clean all those years in the dusty desert, but once they reached the rivers of Canaan. . . "Okay boys, it's time for a scrub! Wash them armpits! Wash them clothes!" These days, unless you're out camping, you don't need to wash your clothes yourself. Your washing machine will do that for you. (Mom would be happy to if only she could *find* the dirty duds.) But one thing you can and must do is bathe yourself.

Don't wait till you're so stinky that you kill roses simply by walking past them. Bathe regularly. And bathing doesn't mean lying in a sudsy tub blowing bubbles and playing with the rubber ducky. Sure, take the goggles in if your parents let you, but just remember this: To get clean you have to use soap, you have to scrub the grime off your body, and you have to shampoo your hair.

Wash up often. Be considerate of other people's noses. . .and the roses.

devotion #14

GIRLS ARE COOL

There is neither . . . male nor female, for you are all one in Christ Jesus.

— Galatians 3:28

Many ancient peoples — including Israelites — looked down on women. That's the way it was back then. In ancient days, a woman's word really didn't count. She couldn't even be a witness in a court case. When Jesus came along, he put that attitude out on the curb with the recycled trash. Instead of putting women down, Jesus showed the world how important they were. Did you know that the very first people to witness that he had been raised from the dead were women? It's true!

Paul is saying don't judge people by whether they're male or female. Now, that doesn't mean that men and women are the same. They're different, to be sure, but men are not better than women. They're equal. Yet even today some boys think they're cooler than girls. They say stuff like, "Boys rule, girls drool." Listen guys, toddlers drool, *Jesus* rules, and both boys *and* girls are cool.

No sweat if you'd rather hang out with guys than girls. Boys are interested in boy stuff, so that's perfectly normal. But the thing is, you gotta treat girls with respect. That doesn't mean you need to like all the things that girls like; no one's asking you to paint your fingernails. Let girls do girl stuff. That's their thing. Just don't look down on them for it.

Girls are different than boys — no one's arguing with that — but Jesus loves both guys and gals the same! That's the bottom line.

devotion #15

NOT COOL!

A drunkard staggers around in his vomit.

— Isaiah 19:14

In Bible times, beer and wine were plentiful. Like today, some people had no control over their drinking once they started. The first cupful was followed by a second and a third until they got so drunk they were down on all fours barking like a dog. Some were even staggering around and vomiting on themselves and anyone else who happened to be near them.

Sometimes you hear teens say, "You shoulda seen Billy at the party. He was so drunk he was pukin' over the rail. Then he fell off the back porch and rolled around in his vomit." Everyone laughs, and Billy stands there grinning. He imagines the other kids are thinking, "Wow! How cool! What a man!" Hello? Wallowing around in your own foul-smelling whitewash is cool? Some people's definition of a fun time is pretty weird.

Whatever your parents think about alcohol, or whatever your church's doctrine is on wine, *you* must definitely *not* touch it. It's against the law for kids to drink alcohol. So what if some so-called friends mock you for saying no. You have nothing to prove to them. In fact, if they pressure you to drink, ditch them. You go your way and let them go their way.

There's nothing grown-up or macho about kids drinking and staggering around in their half-digested dinner barf. So avoid that whole scene.

Devotion #16

EYE GARBAGE

I will set before my eyes no vile thing.
—Psalm 101:3

The *vile thing* in this verse is not broccoli cooked in sour goat's milk. Back in Old Testament days when the Israelites wandered away from God, they often ended up worshiping false gods like Baal or Asherah. The people built on the hilltops huge stone idols of these gods, and for convenience, they bought themselves a Barbie-sized idol made out of clay or wood. Then they set this *non*-action figure on a shelf in their house so they could see it, kiss it, and pray to it all day long.

These days, setting a vile thing before your eyes could be reading a sick comic book or watching a horror movie that gives you nightmares. It could be playing video games filled with occult images and witchcraft. It could be going on the Internet and seeing stuff that puts

strange thoughts in your brain. When you see negative stuff, your mind takes mental photos of it. Then you have those pictures stuck in your head for months or years.

If you want to avoid seeing endless reruns of sick images, avoid looking at them in the first place. Don't even have them in your house. The Bible warns, "Do not bring a detestable thing into your house" (Deuteronomy 7:26). If a vile thing isn't in your house, you won't be tempted to try hiding it under your mattress.

Don't waste time looking at vile eye garbage. Don't bring it home. If you have it already, put it out with the trash where it belongs.

devotion #17

ROLL UP YOUR SLEEVES

The people of Zebulun risked their very lives; so did Naphtali on the heights of the field.

—Judges 5:18

Long ago a Canaanite king named Jabin conquered northern Israel, and for twenty years he cruelly oppressed them. Finally, a warrior named Barak sent out an urgent message to all the tribes of Israel to gather an army and defeat the Canaanites. Only problem was, some tribes, like Zebulun and Naphtali, faced the full heat of the battle while others, like Reuben and Dan, didn't even bother to show up.

Afterward, the Israelites had years to sit around, roll up their sleeves to show off their battle wounds, and talk about the heroic fighting that day. But those who *didn't* show up also had years to ask themselves why they *weren't* there when they were needed. It's the same today if your youth group is on a major fund-raiser, and you opt out; or your parents ask everyone to help clean the house, but you skip out and play video games.

There will be times in your life when people will be counting on you to be there. Decide ahead of time that you'll answer the call, roll up your sleeves, and help. Jesus said that if you love others, you'll lay down your life for them. That doesn't only refer to dying on a battlefield. It could simply mean being there and helping out — especially if you promised that you would.

There are opportunities every day for a man to do what a man should do. Let every day be your moment of truth.

Devotion #18

BURST OF POWER

The Spirit of the LORD came upon him in power so that he tore the lion apart with his bare hands.

—Judges 14:6

You've heard of Samson, the super strong guy—rippling muscles, flowing long hair. Well, one day he was walking along the road when this ferocious roaring lion leaped out. Then it was like King Kong wrestling T. rex, only Samson didn't just snap its jaw, he *ripped the cat apart*! You know what that's like: you go to open a bag of chips and accidentally tear the bag apart and chips end up all over the floor. Well, in this case it was lion guts spilling out.

Samson probably had a well-cut body, but you gotta know his strength went *way* beyond what normal mus-

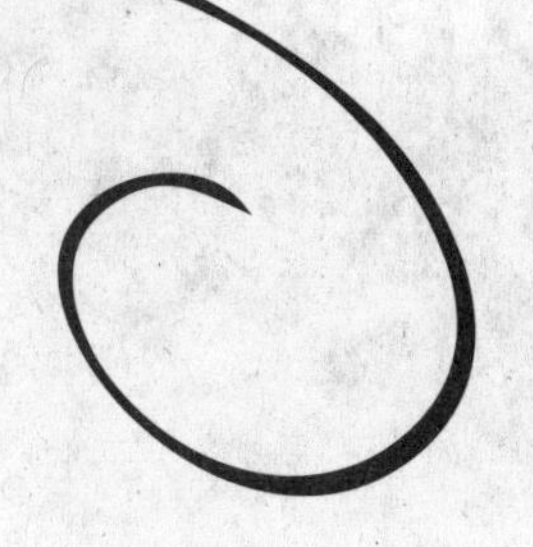

cles do. So where did all this superpower come from? "The Spirit of the Lord came upon him in *power*." Cool! You're probably wondering, "Is all that good stuff gone?" Well, odds are that the Holy Spirit won't make you as strong as Samson, but God knows there'll be times when you *do* need extra bursts of strength.

So, your body comes fully loaded with adrenal glands. In emergencies these little doo-dads dump power juice called adrenaline (ah-*dren*-ah-lin) into your blood, and for a few seconds or minutes, dude, you have far greater strength than you normally have. It's like the jet engines of Batman's car kicking in. Don't expect to twist steel girders, but in real emergencies the power's there for you. (Ta-daaa! It's Adrenaline Man!)

Talk about wonders of the human body! God thought of everything!

devotion #19

ENDURANCE

Joshua waged war against all these kings for a long time.

—Joshua 11:18

If you read the book of Joshua, you get a wide-screen picture of knockout battles, surprise attacks, and huge military victories. But that all happened during the first couple of years of the move into Canaan! Joshua waged war for another four years *after* that, and by then the Canaanites had dug in. They oiled their chariot wheels, opened new sword factories, and added extra bricks to their walls. Then the war bogged down, and the Israelites sat around besieging cities.

It's not all about being lightning quick with a sword. It's not all about courage and strength. Often you need *long-term* strength. That's called *endurance*. For example, you're excited when you first start taking martial arts lessons but after a while you're bored with all the repetition. You need stick-to-itiveness. Or maybe you take on snow-shoveling jobs in your neighborhood, then after a few weeks think it's just too much work. You need endurance.

Where do you get endurance? You have to make a *commitment*. Joshua and the Israelites were committed to carving out a homeland in Canaan. (They *had* to be! They couldn't just mosey on back to Egypt.) If you're involved in a huge, long-term project, make a commitment that you'll finish it. Then tackle it one day at a time. Do what you can do in one day and leave the rest for tomorrow.

Take a tip from Joshua and set your mind to the fact that for some projects you'll have to "wage war a long time."

devotion #20

STRENGTH FROM INSPIRATION

Blessed are those whose strength is in you,
who have set their hearts on pilgrimage....
They go from strength to strength.

— Psalm 84:5, 7

A *pilgrimage* is when you go on a journey for spiritual reasons, like when the Pilgrims left England to find religious freedom in America. Or it can mean taking a trip somewhere to worship God. Well, three times a year, the Israelites headed for Jerusalem to worship God at the temple there. Some of them had to walk long distances. Sometimes they had to sneak through enemy lines. The Israelites really had to have their hearts *set* on the trip to make it through such obstacles.

If you wake up Sunday morning and find that you're snowed in, unless your heart is *set* on going to church, you probably won't want to help shovel out the driveway. Or if it costs fifty dollars to go to your church's summer camp, unless you're really motivated to go, you won't put out and do chores to earn the cash.

When the Psalm says that you will "go from strength to strength," it doesn't mean that God will miraculously make your muscles bigger. After all, it's up to you to exercise. But God can make you strong in other ways. He gives you the vision for something, you set your heart on it, and you're inspired — so inspired that instead of getting worn out, you're pumped by the time you're done.

Set your heart on serving God, and he'll give you the physical and mental strength to see it through, step-by-step.

devotion #21

BUFF ISN'T ENOUGH

"Let not . . . the strong man boast of his strength . . . but let him who boasts boast about this: that he understands and knows me, that I am the LORD."

—Jeremiah 9:23–24

God had just finished telling the Israelites that disaster was going to hit their land and there was nothing they could do to stop it. The enemy was going to invade their land and smash into their fortresses. The Israelites could boast till they were blue in the face about how strong they were, but they weren't anywhere *near* strong enough to stop what was coming. Only knowing God could protect them.

If you're tough, don't lie and say, "Oh man, I'm not that strong." If you're strong and you *know* that you're strong, have a healthy self-confidence. Know that kids can't push you around. If tough situations come up, be confident that you can face them. There's nothing wrong with that. God wants you to be buff.

But don't go around boasting about how strong you are 'cause no matter *how* tough you are, you can't handle *all* the heavy stuff life sends your way. A lot of things are so big that you can't protect yourself from them. If you depend on your muscles alone, you'll go under. But realize that you have your limits and that you need *God* to protect you, and you'll make it.

God is strongest of all. Jesus has more power in his little finger than you have in your entire body. When you can't handle stuff, trust him to take care of it.

Devotion #22

NOT BEATING THE AIR

I do not fight like a man beating the air.

— 1 Corinthians 9:26

Boxing is a lot tamer now than it used to be. The Greeks and Romans held boxing competitions, only back then boxers didn't wear gloves. They used bare fists. Worse yet, they wrapped hard leather around their hands to cause *extra* cutting damage. Paul obviously spent time watching boxers training and beating the air. See, no one had thought to invent punching bags yet, so Romans were big into shadowboxing.

A boxer has to practice to be prepared, but when it comes time to fight, practice is over; now all his skills are put to the test. It's the same with any sport. In basketball, for example, you practice dribbling and shooting the ball through the hoop. But when you're out on the court, and the crowds are going wild in the stands, you

gotta take what you've learned, slip through the other team's defenses, and make things happen.

Paul used boxing as a symbol of a man of God battling against wicked spiritual forces and said he wasn't just shadowboxing. Even though the forces fighting you are invisible, they're real! You're not just beating the air.

In whatever you do, if you want to excel, you have to practice. But when the real deal comes, it's showtime. No more beating the air. Now the goal is to connect.

Devotion #23

TEMPTATION

Flee the evil desires of youth.
—2 Timothy 2:22

When the apostle Paul was in prison for being a Christian, he wrote a letter to a young friend named Timothy. Paul warned, "Flee the evil desires of youth." Now, why did he say *that*? Because a Christian named Demas had just been derailed by evil desires. Paul said, "Demas, because he loved this world, has deserted me" (2 Timothy 4:10). We don't know what exactly Demas was tempted by, but it totally stopped him from following Jesus. Paul didn't want Timothy to go down too.

Things like skateboarding, mountain biking, soccer, and swimming are good. There's nothing evil about desiring to do these things. And movies and video games can be cool. But there *are* evil movies and video games that you *shouldn't* desire. And even perfectly normal desires—like a man's desire for sex—can become evil desires if you're not supposed to have them yet.

When it comes to the *good* stuff you love doing, enjoy it. But wait for things you're supposed to wait for and stay away from evil stuff you're supposed to stay away from. You know what kinds of things tempt you, so be on guard. Your parents know too; so if they warn you that you're getting too close, listen to them. Paul watched out for Timothy; your parents watch out for you.

Don't stand there staring at the temptation while you're trying to resist it. Walk away. In fact, if the temptation is strong, flee!

devotion #24

FORTY-YEAR-OLD JEANS

During the forty years that I led you through the desert, your clothes did not wear out, nor did the sandals on your feet.

— Deuteronomy 29:5

The Israelites left Egypt to conquer Canaan, but when they learned about the armies and fortresses they'd have to fight there, they chickened out. God punished them by making them wander in the wilderness for forty years. Um, one small detail: they couldn't buy new clothes out in the desert. Normally, after forty years the clothes would be tattered rags on their backs and their sandals would fall apart, but God kept that from happening.

For forty years — exactly 14,610 days — the Israelites didn't need to

change their clothes. Boys must have loved this! Now, God can still do miracles like that — make clothes extra durable — but he usually doesn't. These days if you wear the same pair of jeans week after week, you'll tear holes in the knees and wear them completely out. And the smell! *Hooweee!*

Unless you're an astronaut marooned on the deserts of Mars, you have no excuse for not taking off your dirty clothes. So change 'em before they get so bad they rot right off you. Or if your clothes are still clean after wearing them a day or so, fold them or hang them up so you can find them in the morning. Don't just drop them on the floor.

Take good care of your clothes and they'll stay looking good and last you a long time. Not forty years, no, but at least until you grow out of them.

devotion #25

SIBLING SOLUTIONS

"Men, you are brothers; why do you want to hurt each other?"

— Acts 7:26

Pharaoh's daughter adopted a Hebrew baby, called him Moses, and raised him as a prince in the palace. But one day Moses found out that he wasn't Egyptian. "Gulp! You mean those. . . Hebrew *slaves* are my people?" Now, Moses knew that the Egyptians were treating the slaves harshly. He expected, naturally, that this would cause the Hebrews to stick close together. Surprise, surprise! He saw them pounding on *each other*! He didn't get it.

How many times does this happen in your home — you and your siblings settling arguments by pushing, hitting, and kicking each other? It's one thing to quarrel and disagree, even to get upset

with each other, but you *shouldn't* take your disagreements into the gladiator's arena. God doesn't give you strength so that you can pound on your brothers and sisters.

Lots of cartoons show superheroes pounding bad guys or guys with giant guns mowing robots down. This can give the impression that "might makes right." It doesn't. Sure, if alien robots invade earth some day, it's probably okay for you to blow them up. But most of the time, men of God don't use force to settle arguments. They listen to the other guy, talk things through, and try to work out a solution that makes everybody happy.

You don't have to be kind to alien robots. But you *do* have to love your brothers and sisters. When you have a quarrel with them, talk things through. Try to work things out.

Devotion #26

WANT RESPECT?

"I chose the way for them and sat as their chief; I dwelt as a king among his troops."

—Job 29:25

Read the whole chapter of Job 29, and you'll see that Job wasn't kidding! He really *was* like the king of Uz. He had humongous power and influence. Job was like the top general, a Supreme Court judge, and a bank president all rolled up in one. And how did Job use this power? To get everybody in Uz to bow down to him? To invade the neighboring kingdom? Nope. He used his position to feed the hungry and give justice to the poor.

As you grow bigger, stronger, and smarter, you find that you can do a lot of things that little kids can't. And it can be real *tempting* at times to use your extra smarts to trick them out of something you want, or to use your muscles to push them around. It's not only tempting but a lot of guys do exactly that. No surprise there.

What's cool is if you use your intelligence to keep little kids from doing dumb stuff, or use your strength to help them do things they can't do on their own. Think of ways you can use your power and influence to help others. Want a sure sign that you're growing up? Help others. Don't just look out for yourself.

Want your younger brothers and sisters to respect you and follow your lead? Be there for them when they need you, and they'll get used to respecting you and listening to you.

Devotion #27

LIGHT-YEARS AHEAD

"Though you soar like the eagle and make your nest among the stars, from there I will bring you down."

— Obadiah 4

God was talking to Israel's enemies, the Edomites, who lived high up in carved-out cliffs like something out of an *Indiana Jones* movie. The Edomites were about to find out how powerful God was. God was *not* saying that the people of Edom had built spaceships and started colonies around distant stars. (They hadn't, by the way.) God was saying that even *if they had* done that, he could still bring them down.

If God can bring down a star colony that's light-years away — and we're not even there yet — we'd better

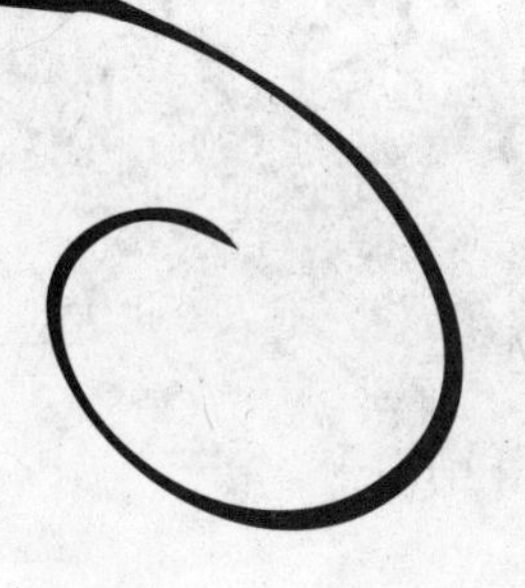

not get a big head. Our cutting-edge technology still doesn't cut it. These days we can get so awed by modern gadgets, powerful computers, and DNA engineering that we sometimes wonder if we really need God. Like the ancient Edomites, we've become overconfident. We think we're standing tall and strong without God.

It just isn't so. Our nation — and each of us personally — needs God. We haven't even got a colony on Mars yet — or even the moon! And even when the day comes and we're there, we'll still need him. Hey, if you join the space program and end up one of the first astronauts to Mars, stay humble.

God is way out there — light-years ahead of all of us — and he's got a *lonnnng* reach. So don't think you have things together without him.

Devotion #28

THE A-TO-Z FACTOR

The race is not to the swift or the battle to the strong... but time and chance happen to them all.

—Ecclesiastes 9:11

King Solomon had done his best to be a fair king and rule well. He had appointed judges all over Israel and ordered them to judge fairly. But he couldn't put an end to all injustice. He couldn't control the weather, prevent freak accidents, or eliminate crime. By the time Solomon was old and had ruled for many years, he came to the conclusion that life wasn't always fair. Good guys didn't always come out on top.

If you practice hard, you may become the best, but you won't necessarily win. Even the fastest runners strain muscles. Even the best figure skaters

fall on their butts doing a triple Axel—whatever *that* is. Even the strongest warriors go down in battle. Now, usually the fastest runners *do* win the race. Usually the best warriors *do* win the battle. . .but not always. There's always the X factor, the uneXpected.

Sometimes you just have to deal with it when you *should've* won, but you didn't. Other times you can avoid losing out by praying to God for protection and help. Remember, he's bigger than the X factor. God is the A-to-Z factor, the Alpha and the Omega. So pray ahead of time for his protection from accidents, X-idents, and other X stuff.

In heaven, things will be perfectly fair and just, but right now we're still living in an imperfect world. So just do your best. . .and pray.

Devotion #29

SPIRITUAL DEFENSES

"Have you not put a hedge around him and his household and everything he has?"

—Job 1:10

When the Devil wanted to attack Job, his big complaint was that he just couldn't get *at* Job. In the spiritual realm, God had put a hedge around Job and his stuff. Now, in Bible days hedges weren't made of pretty green cedars. Think of a hedge of thorns like the *bomas* that Africans used to build around a camp at night to keep lions out. Can't you just picture the Devil trying to get through a thorn hedge and finally backing out, all scratched up?

You simply can't avoid all accidents, sicknesses, and problems. Yet many Christians tell stories about God protecting them when they prayed for protection.

Have you ever taken a major spill on your skateboard or bicycle but walked away with only a few small scratches? Why? Probably someone prayed for you.

Be as strong as you like, but problems can still take you down. That's why you need serious protection. If you stay close to God, he can turn away problems and protect you from trouble. That doesn't mean *nothing* bad will ever happen, but God can stop a lot of grief before it hits. God's protection is like being surrounded by strong bodyguards — or a thorn hedge.

God put up spiritual defenses to protect Job, and he can do the same thing to protect you today.

Devotion #30

STRONG, SILENT TYPE

The stone over the mouth of the well was large. When Jacob saw Rachel . . . he went over and rolled the stone away.

— Genesis 29:2, 10

Esau and Jacob were brothers. Esau was Mr. Hairy-chested He-man Hunter while Jacob was Mr. Quiet Guy. In most Bible storybooks Esau is built like the Hulk and Jacob's a skinny guy. *Wrong*. One time Jacob went to the Haran town well, and along came his cousin Rachel leading a flock of thirsty sheep. A megasize stone lid covered the well, and it was like a two-shepherd job to move it. But our man seized the stone and rolled it away — by *himself*. See, Jacob was strong too. He was just the strong, silent type.

Some guys today have a reputation for being tough, but it's mostly just tough *talk* and pushiness. Sure, they have muscles, but they talk about their arm meat so much that it seems they have more ego than strength. A lot of other kids are strong too, but they're not always bragging about it.

It's great to have muscles, and if you've got 'em — or you're getting them — good for you. Just remember that it takes more than boasts and brawn to succeed at important stuff in life. If you want to do great things, physical strength just isn't enough. You also need to walk with God.

You may not be as strong as Esau *or* Jacob, but you can use your muscles to do good stuff. Oh yeah. . .and don't applaud yourself.

devotion #31

FOLLOW THROUGH

"'Son, go and work today in the vineyard.'
He answered, 'I will, sir,'
but he did not go."
— Matthew 21:28, 30

Jesus told a story about a farmer who had two sons. The farmer said to Son One, "Son, go and work today in the vineyard." Son One grunted no, so Dad told Son Two to take care of the vines. This guy promised, "I will, sir." But *he* never went. Well, *that* was some help! Fortunately, Son One felt so bad about telling Dad no that he went and worked.

Lots of kids are like the second son. They promise, "Sure, I'll do it," but only because saying no would cause trouble. Either that, or they say yes, go right on playing, and forget to follow through. So by bedtime the garbage still isn't out

on the curb, the Lego bricks are still covering the bedroom floor three inches deep, and the dog's so hungry it eats the hamster. And then the son hears his name being called...

Here's how to avoid that scene: when your parents tell you to do something, give them your full attention and listen to what they're saying so you know you got it. Then — unless it's simply impossible — do the chore immediately. That way, the garbage gets put out, the Lego bricks get picked up, the dog gets fed, and the hamster lives.

You get a bad rep with your parents and your friends if you don't follow through on your promises. Be a man of your word. If you promise you'll do something, *do* it.

devotion #32

LIFE CHANGES

After Abraham's death,
God blessed his son Isaac, who then
lived near Beer Lahai Roi.

— Genesis 25:11

Jacob and Esau were young teens when Grandpa Abraham died. Right afterward, their dad (Isaac) moved his family south from Hebron out into the desert. The well of Beer Lahai Roi was the farthest shepherd's outpost; there was nothin' past it but rocks and dust. Isaac and his sons went from a house to a tent, from a bustling town to the last whistle stop before nowhere. See, Isaac had to fulfill his life's mission, and he figured his boys would love the change.

Sometimes your family has to move: your dad gets a job in another city, or you uproot from your old neighborhood and move across town to a new house. It's hard when you can't see your old friends anymore. They might as well be living on Mars for all you get to visit them. Sure, there's email and telephones, but it's still rough leaving friends behind.

Changes are exciting, fun, and difficult all at the same time. When you grow up and leave home, you may move again and again. You'll probably change jobs several times until you find one you like. Right now it's your parents' job to make those difficult decisions, and you have to trust that they're doing what's best for your family.

When a move seems hard to make, or it looks like you're moving from a good situation into a tough one, remember Isaac's family. At least you're not going to a sheepherding station in the desert.

devotion #33

EYEBALLS UNDER CONTROL

"I made a covenant with my eyes not to look lustfully at a girl."

— Job 31:1

When Job got sick and lost everything he owned, his friends came to comfort him. Soon they began accusing him: "Surely you must have sinned *somehow* for God to let all this happen to you." They accused him of this; they accused him of that. None of it stuck. But Job knew what they were thinking — that he must've sinned sexually. Job let them know in no uncertain terms that he had never cheated on his wife. (See Job 31:9 – 12.) In fact, Job didn't even *look* lustfully at other women.

God was the one who invented sex. God was the one who designed men to want sex, but he also had a

plan: men and women are supposed to enjoy this beautiful experience only within marriage. You may not think girls are so attractive now, but as you get older, your hormones will kick in and start bringing about big changes in your body. Then you'll be seriously interested in girls.

That's why it's important to notify your eyeballs ahead of time that you won't look at girls with lust — not even at girls in magazines. Why? Because Jesus said that if you look at a woman that way, you've already committed the sin in your heart. So don't go there. Put a channel lock on your eyes.

Keep your eyeballs under control like Job did, and it'll be a lot easier to keep the rest of your body in line.

Devotion #34

MOTIVATED TO WORK

"When he sees . . . how pleasant is his land, he will bend his shoulder to the burden."

— Genesis 49:15

Thousands of years ago a guy named Jacob had twelve sons. When Jacob blessed his sons, he compared his son Issachar (*Issa*-car) to a donkey. A donkey is a strong beast that — if it is motivated — can work hard and carry heavy saddlebags. Issachar liked to lie around resting as much as the next guy, but when he caught the vision of how good life could be if he worked, he put out.

It's the same today. A newspaper route is hard work. You can't sit at home watching TV if it's time to walk the block delivering papers. So what motivates you to get off the couch, strap on

your skates, and pull your cart full of papers down the street? Money, and the good stuff it can buy, makes it worth it.

Hard work is just that — hard work — but it's worth it. Maybe your parents and grandparents give you stuff now, but the older you get the more you have to start earning your own way. And in the world out there, you don't get something for nothing. Maybe you'd rather play on the Xbox than mow the lawn, but unless you find a way to raise cash, you won't be able to buy the new game when you've defeated every level in the old one.

Do you need cash to buy some cool stuff? Then find some paying jobs and "bend your shoulder to the burden."

devotion #35

LOCK IT UP!

He built up the fortified cities of Judah, since the *land* was at peace. No one was at war with him during those years.

— 2 Chronicles 14:6

What's King Asa doing? No one's attacking him. Everything's peaceful, and this dude is building fortresses all over Judah. Well, there was trouble everywhere *else*. "All the inhabitants of the lands were in great turmoil. One nation was being crushed by another" (2 Chronicles 15:5–6). Asa figured that it was only a matter of time before trouble came *his* way. Good thing he *did* get prepared, because when a huge army invaded, Asa was ready. He trusted God and won the battle.

Why do your parents lock the doors of your house if it's never been broken into? Why do they set burglar alarms? Why do they lock the car doors? Come to think of it, why do you have a combination lock on your school locker or a chain on your bicycle wheel?

Okay, okay, so you know that you need a lock on your locker or your stuff will get stolen. And it's a no-brainer that an unlocked bicycle disappears. Well, that's the same reason your parents insist on safety stuff. That's why your dad insists that you lock the doors. It may not seem like a big deal, but you'd be surprised at how much grief those kinds of things can save your family.

Don't get sloppy with those details. Those "dumb details" — together with smart prayer — are what keep your family safe.

Devotion #36

SHARK...MUST...EAT

They are like brute beasts, creatures of instinct . . . and like beasts they too will perish.

— 2 Peter 2:12

Sharks are strong, fearsome creatures, but they don't have huge brains driving them. They go by instinct. If they're hungry, they kill and rip and gulp until they've filled their gut. Ever seen nature shows with sharks going wild in feeding frenzies? They're not thinking of the needs of the shark next to them. They're only looking out for themselves. Their thinking goes like this: *Shark . . . is . . . hungry. Shark . . . must . . . eat.* The apostle Peter talked about guys like that. He called them "brute beasts."

Some guys today live their whole lives in a self-feeding frenzy. They push to the front of the line and grab the biggest piece of birthday cake. They rush home from school, shove their sister aside, grab the video game controller from her hands, and shout, "*I'm first!*" They're looking out only for piggy number one.

When you pause and think of other people's needs — not just your own — you stop being self-ish. You've stopped going just by instinct, and you've started caring about others. The Bible says to love your neighbor as yourself. Do that, and suddenly you're wondering if the next guy is hungry or if he has had his turn at a game.

Learning to think of others' needs is part of growing up. It's a sign that you're maturing and becoming less like a shark and more like a man of God.

devotion #37

TURN THE OTHER CHEEK

"If someone strikes you on the right cheek, turn to him the other also."

— Matthew 5:39

Jesus said that if someone strikes you on the cheek, don't start fighting. In fact, offer him your other cheek too. Now, many Christians think this means that if someone starts slugging you, you're supposed to *let* him keep punching your teeth in. Even if he's beating you to a pulp, you're not supposed to defend yourself. *Wrong!* When Jesus said strike, he used the Greek word *rhapizein*, which means "to slap". You don't usually get hurt from a slap. It's more of an insult than anything.

If you're hotheaded and someone insults you, you probably start screaming insults back. If you lose your temper easily, other kids may have fun provok-

ing you into shouting matches and fights. Don't let them. That bozo with a big mouth isn't taking anything away from you. Don't let him egg you into fights.

If someone's insulting you, it's a reflection of *his* bad attitude. He may act that way because he has low self-esteem and is trying to feel better about himself at your expense. Letting it pass is a sign of strength. But if someone actually starts slugging you, don't hesitate to defend yourself by telling an adult. Assault (attacking someone) is a crime; it's against the law.

Be patient toward immature kids and show them God's love. That is called "turning the other cheek." But make sure they understand that they can't just walk all over you.

devotion #38

READY FOR ROUGH TIMES

"You know your father and his men; they are fighters, and as fierce as a wild bear . . . your father is an experienced fighter."

— 2 Samuel 17:8

Young hotshot Prince Absalom had just taken over the kingdom in a surprise attack, and now he wanted to chase King David and finish him off. An old man named Hushai gave Absalom a reality check. He reminded Absalom just how tough his dad and his men *were*: They were strong and fierce and they had fought dozens of wars. Bottom line: think twice before you mess with *these* guys. Hard experiences had made them tough.

You may be going through hard times right now. If you are, you're probably not too interested in the fact that it's making you tougher. You just want things to be *easier*. ("I'll get tough some *other* way. Yeah, like by eating raw marshmallows.") Well, you often can't choose what comes your way. Usually you have to endure hardships, like it or not.

The upside is that tough times really *do* make you tougher. Then when you face major problems, you're mentally prepared. You're not fazed if your plane crashes in the Alaskan wilderness and you have to hike out, hopping on one foot. Okay, maybe not *that* extreme. But being ready to rough it can make all the difference. It means you'll still be standing when the hard times pass.

Sometimes you feel like groaning when you experience tough stuff. Don't overdo the groaning. Like King David, you need enough rough stuff to make you tough.

Devotion #39

HELMETS AND SHIN GUARDS

He also went down into a pit on a snowy day and killed a lion.

— 2 Samuel 23:20

What is this guy *doing*? Talk about risk takers! Okay, so Benaiah, one of King David's greatest warriors, needed to kill this lion for some reason, but couldn't he find a rock to drop on its head? Did he really have to jump into the pit and wrestle it? This is definitely one of those don't-try-this-at-home stunts. Benaiah killed the lion, but try something like that, and it'll be *you* getting killed.

Probably when your dad was a boy, there were no laws stating that kids had to wear helmets when they rode a bicycle or skateboard. Back then when kids went off a bike ramp and came down head first, serious injuries happened. So now we have the helmet rule. Ever feel it's too much trouble to strap on your helmet, elbow-guards, and knee-guards? It's not. Look at the bumps on your dad's head. (*Juuust* kidding.)

You'll face enough dangers in your life that you can't avoid, so no need to rush into danger you *can* avoid. Crack your skull by riding without a helmet, and you won't be there when you need to save some kid's life. For what it's worth, Benaiah was probably wearing a helmet when he jumped into the lion pit — an army helmet, that is.

Sometimes you simply have to take risks that can't be avoided. But in the meantime, strap on the helmet and wear protective padding.

devotion #40

LUST OF THE EYES

Everything in the world — the cravings of sinful man, the lust of his eyes . . . comes not from the Father but from the world.

— 1 John 2:16

Tons of magazine and TV ads show pretty women selling something while dressed in almost nothing. What's the big idea? Can't they afford clothes? Oh, yeah, they can. Those bikinis are their *work* clothes. See, automobile companies and other advertisers want to get men's attention, and since they know that guys are interested in sex, the advertisers bring on the beach babes.

This is why there are "men's" magazines on the racks and "adult" channels on TV. All these X-rated images that feed the "cravings of sinful man" and the "lust of the eyes" are

called *pornography*. (*Pornography* comes from the Greek word *porne*, which means "to sell sex for cash.") Now, it's fine to notice that a girl is beautiful, but the problem with staring at porn is that it gets your mind working overtime, craving sex — and that leads to trouble.

God loves human beings. To make *sure* humans keep having children, God programmed men to be very attracted to women, and he made sex very enjoyable. But here's the deal: God wants you to enjoy sex *within marriage* — not before marriage, not outside of marriage. To be sure you got that point, he spelled out some rules in the Bible. Obey them and you'll steer clear of problems.

Make up your mind that you'll honor God by keeping your eyes away from pornography. Stay away from X-rated magazines and videos.

Devotion #41

READY TO DEFEND

"Fight for your brothers,
your sons and your daughters,
your wives and your homes."
— Nehemiah 4:14

Nehemiah and the Jews were busy rebuilding the walls around Jerusalem when they heard that their enemies were plotting an attack. Nehemiah immediately posted guards and prayed for God's help. When the threats intensified, Nehemiah put *half* his men on guard duty. He even had the builders wear swords while they worked. And get a load of this: the men who carried building materials worked with one hand and held a sword in the other. (Careful passing me those bricks, Jeb!)

The good news is, because Nehemiah's men were ready to defend themselves — and because they prayed — they never even had to fight. Their cowardly enemies didn't dare attack. They huffed and they puffed, but it was mostly just bluff. Isn't that just like bullies today? They enjoy picking on smaller kids, but when someone their own size stands up to them, they slink away like a walking spring toy going down stairs.

If someone insults you and you let it pass, good for you. Way to go. But when a bully begins pushing around or hurting your little brother or sister, it's time for you to stand up and speak out. Of course, the *best* thing to do is to tell an adult — and pronto! But if there are no adults around, you gotta protect your loved ones.

Be prepared to defend yourself and your brothers and sisters, but pray that it never actually comes to that. It usually won't.

devotion #42

ABSOLUTE PURITY

Treat . . . younger women as sisters,
with absolute purity.
— 1 Timothy 5:1 – 2

Paul's advice to young men was straightforward: respect everyone. Respect older men as if they were your dad and older women as if they were your mom. Treat the guys in your church as if they were your brothers and the girls as if they were your sisters. Of course, all these people don't live in your house with you, but they are part of your *spiritual* family. And this verse focuses on treating *girls* with respect.

Of course, Paul's advice won't make sense if you punch your sister or tease her. "Yeah," you say, "but my sister teases *me*. Am I supposed to be kind to her when she bugs me?"

Well, if she does that, talk to your parents about it and let them deal with her. In the meantime be patient and kind to your sister. Then turn around and treat *all* girls the same way.

And don't forget the "with absolute purity" part. Girls are special people created by God. They're not sexual objects to make dumb jokes about. Don't hang around with guys who make sick comments about girls, otherwise you'll end up spewing out their same brain garbage. Tell them to cut it out, and if they don't, then you cut out of there.

If you respect someone, you don't say bad things about him or her. You don't even *think* bad things about them. That's the attitude God wants you to have toward girls.

Devotion #43

DEFEAT YOUR GIANTS

"You yourself heard then that the Anakites were there . . . but, the LORD helping me, I will drive them out."

— Joshua 14:12

When the Israelites left Egypt for Canaan, Moses sent twelve spies ahead to check things out. Those guys came back shakin', saying that there were giants in the land — Anakites! No way could they conquer them! Only Caleb and Joshua believed they could. The unbelieving Israelites had to wander in the desert for forty years until a new generation was ready to invade Canaan. The giants were still waiting, but Caleb believed that — with God's help — he could tromp them. And he did.

Are there giants in your life stopping you from entering *your* promised

land? Do huge doubts make you afraid to try out for a sports team? Are you afraid to be downstairs alone? Do you worry that some giant monster is hiding in a closet? Does it seem like way too much work to finish your science project?

Listen. If God wants you to do something, then you can overcome the giants in the way — no matter how big they are. Whether you're staring at a nine-foot-tall Anakite or facing your worst fears, God can help you. You *can* jerk open that closet door or try out for that team or put together a huge science display — whatever.

God helped Caleb defeat the giants when others didn't have the faith for it. Your problem may be too gigantic for you alone, but it's not too big for you and God together.

Devotion #44

HAMSTER-CAGE BREATH

"My breath is offensive to my wife; I am loathsome to my own brothers."

—Job 19:17

A long time ago, a guy named Job lived in the land of Uz. We don't know exactly what kind of sickness Job came down with, but painful sores broke out all over his body. Flies laid eggs in his sores and soon maggots began crawling there. The man looked loathsome. (That means disgusting and revolting.) People dodged him when they saw him in the street. Poor Job was so sick that his breath smelled like the bottom of a hamster cage.

Where does bad breath come from? Well, millions of bacteria called plaque (plak) live in your mouth. They like to feast on the food rotting between your unbrushed teeth, and they especially like to live in the roomy condominiums on the back of your tongue. When they're dead and dying, bacteria release a sulfur compound. That's what causes the stink. Take a look in the mirror. Is your tongue a bit white? That's your own personal bacteria graveyard.

To get rid of these filthy creatures, you need to brush your teeth — and that doesn't mean racing 100 miles per hour down the back rows then speeding across the front. It means cruisin' nice and slow. And don't forget to run your toothbrush over your tongue to get rid of the plaque there. Then rinse your mouth with germ-killing mouthwash. This is *war*, man!

If you don't want your breath to stink like a bacteria compost pile, brush your teeth — and your tongue.

devotion #45

FEARFULLY MADE

I praise you because I am fearfully and wonderfully made.

— Psalm 139:14

When David praised God for the way God had made him, he used the word *fearfully* as in *awesomely* or *amazingly* — not like "Whoa! I look like King Kong!" Another guy named Job asked God, "Did you not. . .curdle me like cheese, clothe me with skin and flesh and knit me together with bones and sinews?" (Job 10:10–11). Job was not complaining that he smelled like sour cheese or that God had sewn him together like Frankenstein's monster. Job just had a funny way of saying, "Thanks for making me the way you did, God."

Maybe you're one of those guys who look in the mirror and go, "Oh yeah! *You* are one good-lookin' dude!" Hopefully not. Chances are that you're not Mr. Perfect and you don't like your whole package. Maybe you're too fat or too skinny for your liking or too short or too tall. Maybe your nose is too big or too small, your teeth are not perfect, and you have a freckle on your eyelid.

Welcome to the real world. None of us is perfect — not even that kid over there, smiling at himself in the mirror. God made you the way you are, and he doesn't make junk. True, he may have had some original ideas. Praise him for the way he made you; you're one of a kind (well, unless you're an identical twin).

Bottom line: accept yourself even if your body is not as perfect or good-looking as you'd like it to be.

devotion #46

CONTENT WITH WINNING

"You have indeed defeated Edom and now you are arrogant. Glory in your victory, but stay at home! Why ask for trouble?"

— 2 Kings 14:10

King Amaziah of Judah had just finished defeating ten thousand Edomites. Way to go! But after that huge victory, he became so proud that he got the idea that he was the original Terminator. That's when he decided to pick a fight with King Jehoash of Israel. Jehoash tried to talk him out of it, but Amaziah wouldn't listen and attacked. . .and Jehoash tromped him. For the next ten years, Amaziah cooled his heels in an Israelite prison.

Some kids win an arm-wrestling match and begin to think that nothing can stop them. They swagger around, picking fights. Sometimes they win, sometimes they lose; but more often than not a teacher breaks it up, and they end up in detention or suspended from school. If they keep doing that when they're older, they'll end up in prison — like Amaziah.

If you win a wrestling competition, advance to the next level in karate — or whatever — stick the trophy on a shelf, hang the ribbon on your wall, show it to family and friends, and be content with that. Use your strength for good, and you're a hero. But use your strength to push others around, and you're just an ordinary bully.

Jehoash's advice was smart: "Glory in your victory, but stay at home!" If you're strong — great! Just don't *look* for trouble by trying to prove how tough you are.

devotion #47

LIVE LONG AND STRONG

Moses was a hundred and twenty years old when he died, yet his eyes were not weak, nor his strength gone.

— Deuteronomy 34:7

Figure *that* one out! You can understand Moses living to be that old — lots of Bible people lived long lives. In fact, today some people live to be nearly a hundred twenty. The thing is though, usually by the time people reach even one hundred, they're wearing glasses and hearing aids, the teeth come out at night, and they're shuffling around with a walker.

So what was Moses' secret? Was he in good shape because he was like a toy that had never been taken out of its original packaging? Nah. Moses had been through the rough-and-tumble of life, including eighty years in the desert.

In fact, that was part of his secret. A lifetime of fresh air, hard work, and eating natural food kept him healthy and strong.

It's the same with you: the way you live now affects how strong you'll be when you grow up. You don't build strong bones and muscles lying on the couch chewing chocolates. Only superheroes get megamuscles when spiders bite them or radiation zaps them. It won't work for you. If you want to be strong, you gotta eat good food, exercise, and get to bed on time.

God designed your body so that if you take good care of it when you're young, it'll still be strong and healthy when you're older. You may not live to be a hundred twenty, but hey, it's bound to help.

devotion #48

TOO MUCH OF A GOOD THING

If you find honey, eat just enough — too much of it, and you will vomit.

— Proverbs 25:16

The ancient Israelites weren't big into raising bees, so bees were wild back then. If they wanted some honey, they had to go look for a beehive — out in the forest or among the rocks. Since Israelites didn't eat honey often, no wonder some guys completely pigged out on it when they found a stash. *Not* smart. Too much of a good thing, and they were vomiting up honey-flavored puke.

These days it's not so hard to find honey. It's usually near the jam in aisle eight. In fact, the shelves have tons of sugary stuff like cereal, soda pop, candy, chewing gum, chocolate bars, syrup, juice, and cakes — not to

mention doughnuts smothered with gallons of glaze! We are a sugar society, and most North Americans eat as much as an entire bathtub full of sugar each year. No wonder some kids get hyper. Worse yet, this constant craving for candy causes cavities as colossal as caves.

It's okay to have a sweet tooth once in a while, but the danger is if you like sugary foods *so* much that you barely want to eat *regular* food. So take it easy on the sweets. Wolf down the good stuff like meat, veggies, and bread, and treat yourself to candies only once in a while. And remember to brush your sugar-covered teeth.

God invented honey, chocolate, and sugarcane so he obviously wants us to enjoy *some* sweets, right? Just don't overdo it, or you'll be down on your knees puking in the toilet.

devotion #49

BATTLE LOST TO THE BOTTLE

Ben-Hadad and the 32 kings allied with him were in their tents getting drunk.

— 1 Kings 20:16

It's a bad idea to be sitting around anytime getting drunk as skunks, but this was a *particularly* bad time for Ben-Hadad, king of the Arameans. At this very moment, the army of Israel was marching out to fight Ben-Hadad's army. The Israelites were hugely outnumbered, but at least they were sober. Ben-Hadad's *army* was ready to fight, but the problem was that Ben and the thirty-two wino-kings were so smashed they couldn't lead the battle — so their armies lost.

Alcohol still causes huge losses these days. Talk about wasted finances! Some guys spend thousands of dollars a year on booze. Alcoholism can wreck a successful career, make a mess of a

marriage, and break up a family. Drunk driving causes many deaths, and — sad to say — quite a few drunk drivers are teens. What are teens *doing* drinking?

Alcoholism is a huge problem in America today, so don't you be the next casualty. Don't experiment with liquor no matter how much the other kids tease. Just say no to the bottle and mean it. Come to think of it, don't even hang around with kids who abuse alcohol. They'll *constantly* be pressuring you to start drinking, and who needs that?

You have your whole life ahead of you. Make the most of it. Don't blow the whole thing like Ben-Hadad and his drinking buddies who lost the battle to the bottle.

devotion #50

IN IT FOR THE LONG HAUL

Let us throw off everything that hinders and the sin that so easily entangles, and let us run with perseverance the race marked out for us.

— Hebrews 12:1

This verse compares Christian life to running a race — a *long* race that is. In fact, it's such a long race that it'll take your whole life to run it. It's not like a hundred-meter sprint to glory. It's more like the Boston Marathon. You wouldn't expect to win that race if you carried a TV on your back, right? So throw off every weight that hinders you.

Paul also said, "I do not run like a man running aimlessly" (1 Corinthians 9:26). It's not like you're going wild, scrambling through a corn maze, and trying to figure out where the path is. In this race the path is marked out for us. The Bible marks the boundary lines clearly — *real* clearly. But the race is long, so you need to persevere (per-se-*veer*). That means "to keep at something, stick to it, and not give up."

How do you persevere? By keeping your eyes focused on Jesus. Jesus is standing at the finish line, waiting to give you the prize. Also remember that Jesus ran this race already and didn't let anything stop him. Now he's sending his Spirit to help you — so don't give up!

Keep your eyes focused on Jesus — keep your eyes on the prize — and that'll give you the perseverance you need to run the race.

devotion #51

STRENGTH WITH MERCY

"Today, though I am the anointed king, I am weak, and these sons of Zeruiah are too strong for me."

— 2 Samuel 3:39

The sons of Zeruiah (Zer-roo-*eye*-ah) were strong, brave warriors who were King David's cousins. All good so far. But there was a problem: these bozos were out of control. David was a strong king, and he wanted to rule with justice and mercy. Not Joab and Abishai, the sons of Zeruiah! When people got in their way — *WHAM*! Their answer to problems was to run a sword through some guy's guts. One day, Joab killed a righteous man named Abner. David was so sick over it that he felt weak.

What's your reaction when some kid plops down and starts playing with one of your toys? Do you rip it out of his hands and punch him? What do you do if your sister's teasing you and won't stop? Do you kick her or pull her hair? C'mon, guys, you *know* that's not the solution. Besides, it'll just get you in trouble.

The problem with Zeruiah's sons was that they were convinced that their cause was *so right* that they were justified in doing whatever they had to do. Not. There are godly ways to deal with problems. Look at King David. He was no pushover, but he knew that strength had to be controlled by mercy and wisdom or it could do more damage than good.

Control your temper and avoid the punch-and-pound solution. Try mercy. You'll be a lot happier and spend less time being lectured.

Devotion #52

YOUR PERSONAL TRAINER

Train yourself to be godly. For physical training is of some value, but godliness has value for all things.

— 1 Timothy 4:7–8

Physical training is of *some value*, all right! Exercise and self-discipline do good stuff for your body, making you stronger, faster, and better at sports. Whether you have a personal trainer advising you how to zing the badminton birdie low over the net, a guy beside the pool showing you how to swim faster than a piranha, or a martial arts instructor teaching you how to block a punch, it's all good.

When you train, you improve your technique — slide into home base sneakier, slice through the water faster, or kick through a brick wall harder (just kidding). You learn about mistakes you've

been making and how to improve — pacing yourself to not wear out quickly and cutting down your time.

The apostle Paul compared sports training to living a Christian life. It takes the same self-discipline and the same focus on the goal — only the results are better than a trophy. If you always try to do the right thing, you become a better person all round. By the way, you have to "train yourself to be godly," but you don't have to do it alone. God is your trainer, and he's always with you.

Just as physical training is good for your physical health, spiritual training is good for your spiritual health and your whole life! Do your best — both in sports and in your walk with God.

devotion #53

WEAR YOUR CLOAK

"When you come, bring the cloak that I left with Carpus. . . . Do your best to get here before winter."

— 2 Timothy 4:13, 21

For thirty years, the apostle Paul traveled around preaching the gospel. Then — *WHAM!* — he was arrested and slammed into the Mamertine Prison in Rome. His cell was a damp underground dungeon with rats. Worse yet, winters in Rome can be cold, and with miserable weather moving in, Paul wanted his cloak. (Cloaks were like warm, wooly blankets that men draped over their robes.)

Most guys these days don't wear cloaks, but a sweater or a jacket can keep you warm. Depending on where you live, winters in America can be cold so you gotta dress for it. The problem is that some kids think only sissies wear coats in cold weather. They think that if you're tough, you should wear only a T-shirt in the fall; and if you're cool, you should tromp through snowdrifts without a jacket.

That kind of thinking isn't cool — it's cold! It doesn't prove you're a man if you get chilled and then stumble around clogged up, sneezing, and with your nose dripping snot like a tap that someone forgot to shut off. All it proves is that kids can talk you into doing dumb stuff. Okay, so it's *not* cool to wear a jacket with cute little mitties safety-pinned to your sleeves, but it *is* okay to put on a sweater or a coat.

It pays to take care of your body. That way you're not at home sick in bed, missing out on some fun or important stuff.

devotion #54

LAME EXCUSES

The sluggard says,
"There is a lion in the road, a fierce lion roaming the streets!"
— Proverbs 26:13

What's this? Lions escaping from the zoo as in the movie *Madagascar*? Well, almost. When flood season hit the Jordan River, rising water often forced the lions living near its banks to find new places to roam. So once in a while a lion might end up near some village. But how come only the lazy guy saw the lion, huh? How come it's the sluggard — the guy who doesn't wanna work — who hears a lion breathing outside? Mighty suspicious.

Lots of kids today make up ridiculous excuses to get out of work. They sound like this: "Put my socks in

the laundry? Oh, did you ask *me* to do that?" Or, "I'm too tired. . .by the way, can I stay up late tonight?" Or, "I didn't brush my teeth because there's no toothpaste. Oh, *here* it is." Or, "Pick up the toys in my room? But I didn't make this mess."

Don't be so lazy that you have to make ridiculous excuses to cover for yourself. Have you noticed how your parents usually don't believe you anyway? You *hope* they're buying your story, but they're just standing there shaking their heads. The solution is to simply do what you're supposed to do. Even if you're in a lazy mood, use some willpower to get yourself up and going.

Just shrug off laziness and do what you're supposed to do. Avoid lyin' around thinking up lion excuses.

Devotion #55

WALKING A LEVIATHAN

"Can you make a pet of him like a bird or put him on a leash for your girls?"
— Job 41:5

Job was a good man — rich and powerful until a whole bunch of bad stuff flattened him. Job wondered why God didn't stop all that bad stuff from happening to him. He felt like he didn't deserve it. God let Job know who was in charge. He reminded Job that he was all-powerful. That's why he asked Job if he could pull a leviathan — a fire-breathing swamp dragon — out of the water with a fishhook. "And Job, once you've caught him, can you lead him like a dog on a leash — without him swallowing you whole?" No can do? Well, *God* can.

Now, guys like to think that they are pretty strong, but they need to get

a grip on the fact that they're not Mr. Incredible. Face it, there are times when you've just done something great and you feel that you're hot stuff. Well, you may be hot, but you're not all-powerful. You're not the most awesome being to walk this planet since T. rex. Next time you "shock and awe" yourself by flexing your muscles, remember how powerful God is.

Or you may groan, "Why doesn't God stop evil-doers?" Remember, God's still in charge. They won't get away with stuff forever. *You* can't stop them, but God's got their number. Stand back, give him time, and let him do his stuff.

You have *no* idea how truly powerful God is. Bear this in mind next time you wonder if God's still around, still strong, and still in charge.

Devotion #56

UNDER PRESSURE

We were under great pressure,
far beyond our ability to endure.
— 2 Corinthians 1:8

The apostle Paul had it so tough in the city of Ephesus, he said he was like a gladiator doing hand-to-hand combat with lions in the arena (1 Corinthians 15:32). Paul was under intense pressure! Sometimes he doubted he'd even survive. Did he go down? No. When troubles hit, he prayed and depended on God more than ever, and God helped him make it.

You know how you feel when your homework or a project comes crashing down on top of you like a tidal wave? You're so overwhelmed that you throw up your hands and groan, "It's impossible!" You probably whine too, but we won't go there. Or you know how wide your mouth hangs open when your dad takes you to the garage on a sunny Saturday and tells you that you have till dinner to finish cleaning it. You get that "gladiator against the lions" feeling.

You only have so much strength, and sometimes you'll be in situations that *are* far bigger than you can handle yourself. Or at least you'll *feel* that the task is so huge that you can't do it. Well, God wants you to learn to depend on *his* strength, not just on your limited strength.

When you feel you can't do a job — it's too big or too difficult — know that with God helping you, you *can* make it.

devotion #57

LIGHTS OUT

Paul . . . kept on talking until midnight. . . . Paul talked on and on. . . . After talking until daylight, he left.

— Acts 20:7, 9, 11

Sound like any sleepover you've been to? You stay up real late talking, and man, you're *dead* on your feet the next day. Well, the apostle Paul had a good reason for talking that long. He had to leave the city the next morning. He thought it was the last time he'd ever see the Christians there, so whatever he had to say, he had to say it then. After talking till the sun came up, Paul headed out on a hike for the next city.

Paul was a tough old crow. He could hack an all-night talkathon then get up and head out on a thirty-mile

walk. But let's face it, most kids can't. God didn't intend you to. So if your parents give you the green light to stay up later than usual 'cause your cousin is visiting from the Congo, go for it. But when they say, "Lights out at ten-thirty," don't keep talking after that.

It can be hard to just lie down and go to sleep when you have someone to pillow fight and tell jokes to. But your parents are the ones making the rules and setting the boundaries. You have to honor them. Besides, Mom and Dad were once kids too. They know that you really do need your sleep.

Have your fun, talk your head off, but know when it's time to shut the blab factory down.

devotion #58

FESTERING INFECTION

"He went to him and bandaged his wounds, pouring on oil and wine."

— Luke 10:34

Remember the story of the Good Samaritan? A Jew was journeying to Jericho when robbers jumped him, grabbed his clothes, beat him up, and left him dying in the dirt. A Samaritan saw the guy lying there and though he didn't know about germs, he *did* know that wounds had to be cleaned. So Good Sam used wine as antiseptic, then poured oil on the wounds, and wrapped them up to keep out the dirt. Smart thinking, Sam!

Boys are usually a lot more rough-and-tumble than girls. You're going to get more than your share of bumps, cuts, scrapes, and bruises. And since so many accidents happen outside in the dirt, germs swarm onto you like Viking raiders, feasting and festering. They breed like crazy, and next thing you know a zillion of them are causing an infection. There are deadly, dastardly diseases in the dirt, so the lick-and-spit trick just isn't good enough.

You don't want to be like a little toddler who needs a bandage on every tiny scratch. On the other hand, don't try to prove you're tough by refusing to get a wound looked after — especially if dirt has gotten into it. And let your mom pour on the antiseptic even if it stings. It's for your own good.

Germs can make you sick. Stop those little losers dead in their tracks. And remember the soldier's motto: take care of your wounded.

devotion #59

SAVE IT FOR MARRIAGE

It is God's will that you should . . .
avoid sexual immorality.
—1 Thessalonians 4:3

Two thousand years ago when boys grew into teens, their bodies went through huge changes. Their glands released a chemical called *testosterone* into their bodies that caused them to become *very* attracted to members of the opposite sex. And the news is testosterone is still doing its thing today. A gorgeous girl walks by and your heart slams around like a basketball, you sweat, and you may even become aroused. Often you can't help *those* reactions, but you *are* in control of what you do next.

As a Christian, you need to exercise self-control and save sex for marriage. Avoid sexual immorality. (That means stay away from breaking God's moral laws on sex.) Now, some teens say, "As long as you *love* a girl, it's okay to have sex with her." No, it's not. Besides, if she gets pregnant, the guy usually ditches her and lets her raise the baby alone. Hello? That's *love*? Moms and Dads who protect and care for their kids — *that's* love.

"Cool" guys brag that they're having sex, but these same guys often get sexual diseases they're *not* bragging about. That includes penis warts and very painful sores called *herpes*. And then there's syphilis and AIDS. Sex outside of marriage is simply not Gods' will. Avoiding immorality *is* God's will.

God knows the problems that sexual immorality causes. That's why he said to avoid it. Just don't do it.

devotion #60

THE TOE THING

The land you are entering to take over is not like the land of Egypt, from which you have come.

— Deuteronomy 11:10

When the Israelites headed to Canaan, God told them what they'd be facing. See, back in Egypt they'd lived on rich land along the Nile River. If they wanted a garden, all they had to do was drop seeds in the dirt, poke the irrigation ditch with their toe, let out some water, and presto! But Canaan was a dry land. The Israelites would have to work hard hoeing the ground and trust God to send rain — either that or lug jugs of water from a well.

Maybe your home is like Canaan. Your parents expect you to work. Instead of picking your shirt off the floor with your big toe, they actually expect you to pick up *all* your clothes! You might even have to feed the dog or vacuum the rug. Is that rough or what?

Maybe other kids do have it easier. Maybe they get away with only doing the toe thing. But by picking up after yourself and helping around the house, you're learning responsibility, self-discipline, and how to be a team player. As you get older and enter the real world, these lessons will put you miles ahead of kids who have it easy now.

Don't grumble if you have to work a little harder than your friends. Good stuff will come from it.

devotion #61

DIRT ALERT!

"Elisha son of Shaphat is here. He used to pour water on the hands of Elijah."

—2 Kings 3:11

The Jews have been scrubbing their hands for thousands of years. In Jesus' day, Mark said that they "do not eat unless they wash" (Mark 7:4). That's already great, but there's more: they not only washed their hands before meals, but made sure the water was clean, running water. They didn't have taps, so folks grabbed a jug and poured water on each other's hands. Elisha was the water boy for Elijah.

You'd think with all the running water in North America today, that boys would be cleaner now than they've ever been, right? Well. . .the dirt on this situation is that most boys still have to be reminded to bathe. Desperately dirty kids have to be shooed into the shower. And washing hands? Some kids use the toilet and then race out of the bathroom without even noticing that the sink exists. Washing before meals? Yeah, *sort* of. . . .

Washing hands means washing hands. The idea is not to get your hands just wet enough so that the dirt smears off on the towel when you wipe 'em. *Scrub* them fingers! Towels were invented to get wet hands *dry*. And while you're at it, do the soap thing. Rub your hands till the bubbles fly.

Elisha's not around anymore to pour water on your hands, but that's not necessarily a huge problem — most homes have running water, so put it to use after toilet duty and before meals.

devotion #62

FEELING OVERWHELMED

"With him is only the arm of flesh, but with us is the LORD our God to help us and to fight our battles."

— 2 Chronicles 32:8

That's King Hezekiah of Judah praying. And he had *good reason* to be praying! Sennacherib, the king of Assyria, had marched in and conquered all of Judah. The only city left standing was Jerusalem, and now nearly a quarter of a million Assyrians surrounded it. Hezekiah said that "only" the arm of the flesh was with Sennacherib. Most guys would've thought, "That's a *lot* of arm! That's a *lot* of flesh!" But Hezekiah trusted God, and that night the angel of the Lord wiped out 185,000 Assyrians.

Sometimes you face situations like that. Not 185,000 Assyrians, no, but maybe your dad loses his job and your family goes through tough times financially. You hear your parents talking, and they're not sure how they'll pay the bills. You want to help, but what can you do? You could sell your toys, but you wouldn't get much for them. Besides, your mom says no. Times like that are when you learn that some problems are too big for you.

The only thing you can do is what King Hezekiah did when his back was against the wall. Pray. The answer might not come immediately. But when things are serious or it's a life-and-death situation, you can pray like Hezekiah did and expect a miracle like he received.

God is still strong today and can still do miracles today to help you — if you trust him. When you feel surrounded, ask God for help.

devotion #63

NORMAL GROWING UP

"When a man has an emission of semen, he must bathe his whole body."

— Leviticus 15:16

As you grow up and become a man... *Oh, wait!* There's a stage between being a boy and being a man, and it's called *puberty* (*pew*-ber-tee). That's when changes begin happening in your body. You start getting hair in funny places, your armpits get BO, your voice gets deeper, you often get pimples on your face, and your testicles begin to produce semen.

That's why it's common for boys around thirteen years old to start having "wet dreams." You're dreaming along and then you dream about someone of the opposite sex. The next thing you know you have an emission

of sperm and fluid from your penis. (An *emission* is something that comes out.) Then you've got sticky wet stuff on your pajamas and body.

You can cut down on this by not putting sexual pictures in your brain in the first place, but the fact is, most young men have wet dreams. It just happens. So besides praying for God to give you pure thoughts, you need to take some practical steps. If you wake up and find that you've had a wet dream, put your pj's or underpants in the laundry, and then take a shower with soap and water.

Stuff like this is a normal part of growing up, so don't freak out. You're not the first boy on the planet it ever happened to. But *do* remember to wash your mind with God's Word and your body with soap and water.

devotion #64

TAKE YOUR BENCH TIME

David went down with his men
to fight against the Philistines, and he
became exhausted.

— 2 Samuel 21:15

When David was a teen, he defeated Goliath. When he became king, he battled the Philistines again. When he got old, he fought them *again*. Like, don't these guys *ever* give up? Well, this last battle went on and on until David was pooped. He couldn't swing that old sword arm anymore. And wouldn't you know it, as soon as he dropped his guard, a giant named Ishbi-Benob came barreling straight toward him. Good thing David's cousin was riding shotgun and took out Big Benob.

It's no sweat if you get tired when you're raking leaves. You sit down for a while and slurp some "brain freeze".

And if you're wiped from too much homework, you take a break, right? Take some downtime to get a drink of water, relax, and think about what you're doing. After a brief rest, you have more energy to play or work again.

But there are times when you really *need* to push, or you're jazzed and *want* to push — like you're in the middle of a game, your team's on a roll, the excitement's high, and you don't want the coach to park you on the bench for a while. If you're excited or afraid, your adrenaline kicks in like emergency fuel and helps you with that last burst of energy. . .but when *that* runs out too, man, you're *really* spent. Then you start making serious mistakes or you trip and injure yourself. So take your bench time. You can only keep going so long when you're tired.

Don't overdo. If you need a rest, take a rest. When you're good to go, *then* get back at 'er.

Devotion #65

PERSONAL BEST

Do you not know that in a race all the runners run, but only one gets the prize? Run in such a way as to get the prize.

—1 Corinthians 9:24

In Roman times, there weren't second- and third-place prizes in athletic competitions. There was only *one* prize, and only the first guy won it. Guess what it was. He got to wear a crown made from *laurel* leaves. Sometimes the crown was made from celery or parsley. Um. . .*okaaay*. But when he arrived back in his hometown, the good stuff happened: They had a parade in his honor; they built a statue of him; and he could eat free forever at feasts.

In your race for God, you're not going for a head decoration made of salad. You're looking forward to the good stuff. Now, angels won't build statues of you in heaven, but you *will* be rewarded beyond your wildest dreams — like feasting with the coolest guys in the Bible.

So how do you get that first-place prize and all the good stuff that goes with it? How you live your life now really does matter. Focus on pleasing God and doing your personal best. Of course, the Christian life is a *long* race. You can't just do a one-time good deed. You need to choose to follow Jesus every day. If you love God, you'll go to heaven — no question about that.

When it comes to sports, schoolwork, or your life for God, do your best and excel.

devotion #66

BE STRONG AND TAKE HEART

My strength fails because of my affliction.

— Psalm 31:10

David was the best king Israel ever had. He was strong, handsome, and crazy about God. He had a huge kingdom and a palace with tons of gold in the basement. David's enemies bowed down and brought him presents when it wasn't even his birthday. Then David made some classic mistakes. His friends turned on him, and his enemies began plotting against him. Dave was emotionally drained. On top of all this, he began having health problems (afflictions).

Ever been so sick with fever or stomach flu that you were physically wasted? Or even if you still *had* strength, you couldn't use it 'cause every time you exerted yourself you felt like vomiting? That's how David felt. And having friends bad-mouth him made him even weaker. David didn't even want to get out of bed. Maybe you've felt that way when a friend turned on you. It's like you're actually sick.

You can't control how friends act, but you *can* put a lid on germs by keeping clean in the first place. And if you're sick, work on getting better. That means if your mom comes along with a huge tablespoon of foul-tasting medicine and says, "Open up," open up. Another thing, stay focused on the good stuff that's happening, not the bad stuff. You'll feel better mentally and physically.

By the end of this same Psalm, Dave figured out the solution. As discouraged and sick as he was, he said, "Be strong and take heart, all you who hope in the LORD" (Psalm 31:24).

Devotion #67

PLUG INTO GOD'S POWER

They were all trying to frighten us, thinking, "Their hands will get too weak for the work, and it will not be completed."

— Nehemiah 6:9

The city of Jerusalem had been in ruins for years and now the Jews were rebuilding the walls. The work was so tough they complained, "The strength of the laborers is giving out, and there is so much rubble that we cannot rebuild the wall" (Nehemiah 4:10). With their physical strength failing, only *willpower* was keeping them going. That's why the Jews' enemies tried to make them afraid and discourage them. If they could shake the Jews' willpower, it'd make them weak.

Ever been faced with a situation like that? You're working hard on a science display and you're *already* frustrated 'cause it's difficult. Then you find you're missing important pieces, and you want to just give up. Or some kid says, "Man, that's *real* sucky-looking!" You feel discouraged and say, "What's the use?" It's like a vacuum cleaner just came along and sucked the strength right out of you.

Fortunately, the Jews had strong faith and believed that God would protect them — and he *did!* That gave them courage, which in turn gave them the strength to keep working. It'll work for you too! There'll be times in your life when you're pooped, discouraged, and afraid; and faith will be the only thing keeping you going.

Trust in God. When you're feeling weak, plug into the electrical outlet of God's power. Faith in God and a can-do attitude can turn the tide.

devotion #68

IMPERFECT PARENTS

But Jether did not draw his sword,
because he was only
a boy and was afraid.

— Judges 8:20

When hoards of Midianites invaded Israel, God told Gideon to gather an army. God then trimmed his army down to a lean, mean strike force of only three hundred men. Gideon and his commandos attacked the Midianites and killed thousands of them. It *had* to be done — it was war — but it wasn't for kids. When they captured two Midianite kings, Gideon had the bright idea to let his son kill those guys. But Jether was only a kid. He couldn't do it.

Some things are for adults only — with good reason — and Jether's dad should've known that this was not a PG-13 activity. War is not for boys. And neither are violent shoot-'em-up video games where you machine gun anything that moves and cyber blood is flying in all directions. And when the label states that a war movie is "rated for mature audiences," that's what it means.

You may wonder why some of your friends' parents let them watch adult movies and play video games designed for older teens. It doesn't matter what standards other parents set for their kids. If your parents have stricter rules, you must honor them — even if they pull a Gideon and allow you to play a certain game or watch a certain video, then later say that it's off limits.

Honor your parents and obey them. They're not perfect, but they're looking out for you.

devotion #69

PROTECTORS OF THE TRIBE

Josiah removed all the detestable idols from all the territory belonging to the Israelites.

— 2 Chronicles 34:33

God raises up Josiah, a strong king down in Judah, when there's no ruler in Israel anymore. Josiah looks around, and he's the strongest kid on the block. No one can stand against him. So how does he use his strength? Does he oppress the Israelites? Tax them? No. The *first* thing he does is smash their disgusting idols and bring them back to serving God.

You have already started doing some serious growing — or you will soon — and you find that you're quite a bit bigger and stronger than younger kids. So how do you *use* your

strength? Do you push your brother or sister around? Do you use your muscles to grab an extra turn on the trampoline? Or do you use your strength to help others?

God gives young men strength for a reason. He meant for men to be the protectors of the tribe. He also meant for men of God to serve him and to help others serve him. So instead of using your mighty superpowers to get your own way, use them to keep younger kids from danger, to stop fights, and to help them to do what's right.

As you grow and become stronger, your mind and your spirit should grow too. When you begin to step up to your responsibility to help others, you're starting to become a man.

devotion #70

USE YOUR GOOD REP

Ahikam son of Shaphan supported Jeremiah, and so he was not handed over to the people to be put to death.

— Jeremiah 26:24

The prophet Jeremiah preached an unpopular message, and the priests and false prophets hated him for it. One day they managed to get their grubby hands on him and decided to do him in. They would've too, except that Ahikam and some other guys spoke up for Jeremiah. Now, Ahikam wasn't Mr. Muscles. He wasn't a soldier. He was just an official, probably a secretary like his dad. But he *was* respected, so he used his rep to protect Jeremiah.

What do you do if you see someone picking on a little kid — teasing him, knocking his books down, or actually pushing him around? You don't want to

get in a fight, right? But what do you do? Just walk on by and not get involved?

If there are no adults around, there are some things you can try. If you *know* the bully, then tell him to stop. If *you're* well known and have a rep, step in and tell him to cut it out. Remind him how lame it is for him to pick on *little* kids. Hopefully he'll listen to you. Of course, if he's hurting the kid, you gotta do more — and tell an adult.

Avoid fights if you can. But if you have any kind of reputation, or say-so, use it to stop kids from hurting or harassing other kids. That's why God gave you a rep.

devotion #71

FEEL OTHERS' PAIN

"He feels but the pain of his own body and mourns only for himself."

—Job 14:22

We feel the pain of our own bodies, that's for sure. God designed us so that if we're cut and bleeding, we can *feel* it and do something about it before all the blood drains out of us. Or if we're sick, we *feel* it and get some rest. In his book *The Gift of Pain*, Dr. Paul Brand explains that pain is actually God's "gift" to us. *Okaaay.*

Newborn babies think only of themselves. If little Sweet Pea has a diaper rash, he could care less if you just broke your leg in a bungee jump. He cares only about his own pain. He's wailing like a cat with his tail stuck in an electrical circuit. Don't laugh. A lot of tween boys are the same.

Mom has a pounding headache, but will they help set the table or carry the laundry basket for her? Nah.

God put *your* pain nerves in *your* body. He doesn't expect you to feel when someone else has pain. But he did happen to supply everyone with mouths and ears, so if someone *tells* you he's in pain, then you know it. And if you care for that person, you want to do something to help him.

One of the surest signs that you're growing up into a man of God is when you start thinking of other people.

Devotion #72

DON'T FALL TWICE

When he was sound asleep, he fell to the ground from the third story and was picked up dead.

— Acts 20:9

The apostle Paul was in an upper room speaking, and this kid named Eutychus (*You*-tea-kus) got the bright idea of sitting on the open windowsill — three stories up. He probably figured that if he breathed some cool, fresh air it'd keep him awake. Nice try. Euty was an accident looking for a place to happen. He nodded off. Down he fell and — *WHAM*! — he was dead. (The fortunate news: Paul prayed for him and he came back to life.)

Lots of accidents happen when you're careless. Here are some scenarios: You don't tie your shoelaces and they get tangled in your bicycle spokes; you're racing through the house to get away from your sister and you slam into your grandma; you step on the marbles you left on the floor and down you go. Even adults get careless and cause accidents. That's why the US Department of Labor (OSHA) has lots of workplace rules.

You can avoid most accidents by obeying commonsense rules — tie your shoes, don't run in the house, and pick up your toys. Sometimes accidents are not serious — you bump your elbow but you're okay. But *some* accidents leave you in pain and badly injured. So while you're having your fun, remember the rules. Play it safe.

After his fall, Eutychus probably didn't go sitting on any more third-story windowsills. He probably figured out a different way to stay awake. Good idea.

devotion #73

YOU KNOW YOU'RE GOOD

As long as he sought the LORD, God gave him success. . . . But after Uzziah became powerful, his pride led to his downfall.

— 2 Chronicles 26:5, 16

King Uzziah was a terrific warrior! He defeated the Philistines and the Arabs, and even the Egyptians sat up and paid attention. Uzziah's army was a powerful force. He fortified cities and had engineers invent new weapons. He figured he was so great that he could break God's law. *WHAM*! Next thing you know this warrior king had leprosy, and all he ruled was the one house he lived in.

If you're really good at some sport and you *know* you're good, fine. If kids come up to you and tell you how good you are, fine. But you're in trouble when you start to lap it all up, 'cause

pride does weird stuff to people's heads. Pride makes you think that the rules that apply to other humans don't apply to you — after all, you're *special*.

Being powerful is not the problem. Getting proud about being powerful is the problem, so steer clear of thinking you're bigger than life. Now, if you *do* get all puffed up with pride, God probably won't strike you with leprosy — or with lightning — but he can find other ways to arrange a face plant and humble you.

Uzziah was such a fantastic king, that it was pretty sad to watch him go down. It didn't have to happen. He could've stayed powerful if only he'd stayed humble. Want to stay on your feet? Don't get a big head.

Devotion #74

PRACTICE MAKES PERFECT

Among all these soldiers there were seven hundred chosen men . . . each of whom could sling a stone at a hair and not miss.

— Judges 20:16

When the seven hundred slingers from the tribe of Benjamin trotted out to battle, the guys coming at 'em had swords, spears, and bows. It *really* wasn't a fair fight. Bows had a pitiful range of only three hundred feet, but a slinger could drop you dead with a man-made meteorite from six hundred feet away. And Benjamite slingers? Ho! These guys were *so* good, they could nail a single hair! Imagine if that hair was on *your* head.

It takes years of slinging to get that kind of range and accuracy. These guys had natural ability, sure, but without practice, they'd never have been *that* good.

Benjy's boys whipped rocks over and over again until they hit a hair every time. It's the same today, whether you're kicking a soccer ball or playing Ping-Pong and trying to *ping* faster than the other guy can *pong*. You gotta do it over and over until it becomes second nature.

You can apply this to your walk with God too. Get in the habit of doing the right thing so that when a temptation comes along, you automatically do what's right. When some little devil ambushes your mind and tries to get you to do the wrong thing, your defenses go up lightning quick and you block his attack.

Practice makes perfect. Well, maybe not perfect, but real good. (We don't need to split hairs over this.) So keep at it. Practice.

devotion #75

BRAND-NAME BLUES

"Why do you worry about clothes? . . .
For the pagans run after all these things,
and your heavenly Father knows
that you need them."

— Matthew 6:28, 32

Back in Jesus' day — just like today — a lot of guys were worried about how they looked. You wouldn't *think* so, considering that they walked around in robes or wore togas that basically looked like short skirts. But hey, they had *their* styles and we have *ours*. They went for togas and sandals; we go for blue jeans and T-shirts.

But seriously, "worry about clothes"? Most boys have to be told to be *more* concerned. They don't give a rip how they look — and as a result, it's their clothes that get ripped. But ever complain that you don't have brand-name runners? Hey dude, you're gettin' into clothes. If you can get the brand name you want, go for it. But if you can't get them and can't bear to face your friends, you're worrying about clothes. . .and running after runners.

Also, as you get older and become interested in girls, you'll find that girls care a *lot* about how guys look. That makes guys image-conscious *reeaaal* quick. Thank God for girls! Just don't get into it so much that you spend all your clothing allowance following fads. God knows that you need good clothes. He's more aware of style than you are. Jesus' point was don't go overboard.

The bottom line is don't get anxious about how you look. What's in your heart is more important than what's wrapped around your outside.

devotion #76

BALANCED MEALS

"Now I urge you to take some food. You need it to survive."

— Acts 27:34

One time a ship carrying 276 passengers, including the apostle Paul, was sailing across the Mediterranean Sea. Suddenly a hurricane-force wind came roaring down on them. For fourteen days the storm blocked out the sun, battering them *violently* in total darkness. The passengers were terrified. They vomited up everything in their guts. They stopped eating and gave up hope. But Paul knew that they were about to crash on the rocks and needed the strength to swim to land, so he said, "Eat."

You probably aren't on a storm-tossed ship, screaming and puking into a hurricane, but the lesson still applies—you need to *eat*. You can't build muscles and stay healthy if you skip breakfast half the time, only snack on a granola bar at lunch, and pick at your dinner. Maybe you're not *that* picky, but do you only go for the starch and meat and skip your veggies?

You need your meat — no beef about that — but you need fruits and vegetables just as much. Remember Daniel and his pals who were shipped off to Babylon? They ate only vegetables and did fine. So chow down on the carrots and peas and corn. Gobble the cukes. Savor the salad. You need the stuff. Doesn't taste so great? At least eat *some*! Your body is screaming for the vitamins they contain.

Yo, man, take some food.
You need it to survive!
Eat the veggies, bite the fruit,
Chew the meat to stay alive!

devotion #77

CUTTING CORNERS

"He is like a man building a house, who dug down deep and laid the foundation on rock."

— Luke 6:48

Jesus talked about two men building houses. The first man dug down *deep* till he struck rock, then laid bricks on that. His house had a solid foundation. Guy Two cut corners. Maybe he was in a hurry to go out and play, or maybe he was just lazy, but — bottom line — doing a good job wasn't a high priority. He plopped his bricks right down on the sand. How smart was *that*? The rains and floods showed up and had fun kicking in *his* little sand castle.

Do you cut corners? Like, when your dad asks you to dig the dandelions out of the lawn, do you go after the roots or do you leave 'em in knowing that they will pop up again next year? When you put your plate in the dishwasher, do you wipe the spaghetti off first? When you clean out the bird's cage, do you *really* clean it or just throw new newspaper on top of the soggy ones?

It takes time to do a good job on your homework or chores, and you'll probably be *reeaaal* tempted to do a quick job so you can run out and play. Nuh-uh. Put in that little bit of extra time to do the job right. That way you don't end up redoing the job later.

Don't be a "sand man" and cut corners. Whatever you do, do it carefully and well. Be like the guy who put in a solid foundation.

devotion #78

TAKING CARE OF YOUR TEMPLE

Don't you know that you yourself are God's temple . . . ? If anyone destroys God's temple, God will destroy him.

— 1 Corinthians 3:16 – 17

A couple thousand years ago, the Israelites traveled to a special building — the temple in Jerusalem — to worship God. Since God dwelled there, people who entered the temple had to make sure that they were right with God before stepping inside. Then Jesus came along and announced that the day of stone temples was done and sent his Holy Spirit into the hearts of all believers! Now *you* are God's temple. Makes you want to be right with God all the time, huh?

Since the Holy Spirit lives inside you, take care of yourself. If you don't, you'll pay the price. That doesn't mean God's going to write your name on a lightning bolt and zap you with a million volts. He doesn't have to. God designed your body so that if you take care of it, it'll usually last a long time. But abuse it by smoking, and you're liable to get cancer. Take drugs — marijuana or crystal meth or whatever — and you'll mess up your body *and* your brain.

If you want to be healthy and strong for a long time, don't smoke or take drugs. That way you can be mountain biking as an old man instead of lying in the hospital with cancer. You can be scuba diving instead of sitting in a drug rehab center. Also, most employers won't hire you if you have a history of abusing drugs.

If you want to do your best and enjoy life to the fullest, keep your mind and your body clean. It's better than self-destructing.

devotion #79

WOMEN ON THE FRONT LINES

Greet Priscilla and Aquila,
my fellow workers in Christ Jesus.
They risked their lives for me.

— Romans 16:3–4

Priscilla and Aquila were Paul's pals, and this husband-wife team worked hard to help him preach the gospel. In fact, they did dangerous, secret-agent-type stuff and risked their lives to help him. Now, have you noticed that in the Old Testament the guys all have names, but often their wives' names aren't mentioned? Yet every time Priscilla and hubby, Aquila, are mentioned, she's not just named, but named *first*. Why? No one really *knows* why. All we know is that Priscilla was one famous, hardworking, gutsy gal.

If you read through the New Testament, you see how many outstand-

ing women there were. Several women even traveled around Israel with Jesus and his disciples. And take a look around next time you're in church. Notice how many women and girls there are? And lots of women are Sunday school teachers and missionaries. Whoa! Women are on the frontlines, doing a *lot* for God's kingdom!

God looks at people's hearts. He's interested in whether you love him and are willing to serve him. You're sitting in church enjoying the ride, but a whole lot of somebodies are working hard behind the scenes to keep things happening. A lot of those somebodies are women.

Women are very important to God. If you still have the idea that girls aren't as cool as guys, it's time to kick that thought out of your head.

Devotion #80

KIDLOCK!

"Jerusalem will be called the City of Truth . . . the city streets will be filled with boys and girls playing there."

— Zechariah 8:3, 5

Jerusalem was in ruins. The Babylonians had battered the walls and burned the buildings. They took the Jews away and enslaved them for seventy years. Finally, the Jews were set free and sent back home, but "home" was a wreck. Jerusalem was so full of rubble and heaps of stones that no one could live there. But God said that people *would* live there once again. And get this! One of the biggest signs of God's blessing was that the city streets would be full of boys and girls playing.

Back then, like now, kids played lots of group sports — kicking balls, playing tag, racing, etc. Since they didn't have any parks or soccer fields, they played in the streets. They literally *filled* the streets! A traffic jam is called gridlock, but this was *kidlock!* These days there are public swimming pools, skating rinks, baseball fields, and other safe places to play. Some kids still play street hockey out on the pavement — on the side streets, that is.

It's fine to play alone, but God knew that it's a whole lot more fun when you play group sports. You'll make more friends and get a lot more exercise. Playing group games means getting out and moving your bod, not just sitting around playing computer games, taking cartoon characters through the levels.

Want to make your city come alive? Want to be living proof that God is blessing the place? Get out and play!

devotion #81

HORSE-SIZED JOBS

"If you have raced with men on foot and they have worn you out, how can you compete with horses?"

— Jeremiah 12:5

That *is* the question, isn't it? If you think track-and-field's tough this year, wait till next year when it's all field and you're up against horses. Seriously though. . .the prophet Jeremiah was complaining that it wasn't fair that he had it so tough while bad men had lives of ease. God basically told Jerry to get ready, "You think it's tough *now*? Wait till warhorses come. The bad guys you think have it so good will be trampled and good guys like you will be on the run."

Maybe you have to drag the trash cans out to the curb every

Thursday. Maybe your mom makes you clean all the Lego bricks off your floor with a snow shovel once a week. Just wait until you have to work eight hours a day at a job you're not crazy about. You think you have a lot of homework now? Wait till you're in college and you have *hours* of homework every night.

Come to think of it, you have things pretty easy right now. The horse-sized jobs and studies haven't even showed up yet, so don't let the small stuff wear you out. Besides, if you have a *can-do* attitude now, that same *can-do* attitude will be there to help you when you're older and things are tougher.

If you think things are too tough, don't just horse around. Instead, remember Philippians 4:13: "I can do everything through him who gives me strength."

devotion #82

BUILDING MUSCLES

Five times I received . . . the forty lashes minus one. Three times I was beaten with rods, once I was stoned.

— 2 Corinthians 11:24 – 25

When the apostle Paul went around preaching the gospel, a lot of people loved him. His message got some people so mad, however, that they beat him. Fortunately, Paul was in *top* physical shape. He took lickings that most men wouldn't have survived and kept on ticking. There were so many whip marks and bruises on his back and arms and legs that Paul couldn't pick one out and tell you where it came from.

That's why the army puts soldiers through boot camp when they join; they want soldiers to be in top shape for when they fight. That's the same reason that you have physical education in your school. Teachers know that kids need gym class to be in shape and healthy. Besides that, physical exercise helps you think more clearly.

Most likely you won't get battered with stones and beaten like Paul, but the Christian life can still be hard. When you do good stuff — like helping some lady from your church move or cleaning up some older folks' yards — you have to be in shape. You're probably too young to be working out in the gym, but another way to get muscles is to faithfully do your chores.

Paul said, "Endure hardship with us like a good soldier of Christ Jesus" (2 Timothy 2:3). To endure hard times, you need hard muscles. To get those you need to exercise.

devotion #83

THANK GOD FOR MONEY

You may say to yourself,
"My power and the strength of my
hands have produced this wealth for me."
But remember the LORD your God, for it is he
who gives you the ability to produce wealth.
— Deuteronomy 8:17–18

God was just about to bring the Israelites into Canaan and give them a rich land full of fruit and grain and luxury stuff like olive oil and honey. Oh yeah, and he was throwing in mines full of iron and copper. All God asked was that when their flocks and herds and wealth increased, they remember to thank him. After all, he was the one giving them this rich land and the strength to make it produce.

God tells you to work because hard work earns money. But if you start getting the idea that it's your strength *alone* that brings in cash, remember who gave you strength and health in the first place. Or if you get paid for doing chores, thank God that your family has a house where you can *do* chores, and that your parents have jobs so they can earn money to pay you.

That's why Christians give money to church. You give part of your earnings back to God to acknowledge that he's the one giving you everything in the first place. If you're thankful to God for your blessings, you show it in a way that counts.

Take a moment to thank God for your health, your strength, and the fact that you either get an allowance or can earn money.

devotion #84

KEEP YOUR COOL

"I your servant had two sons. They got into a fight with each other in the field, and no one was there to separate them. One struck the other and killed him."

— 2 Samuel 14:6

One day a woman from Tekoa showed up in King David's palace with a story from Joab. She told David a parable, saying that she was a widow with two sons. One day her boys were out in the field and began arguing. Then they began fighting. Since no one was there to pull them apart, the fight got out of hand, and next thing you know, somebody was dead.

Ever get in a fight with your brother or sister? First you start by arguing. When no one backs off, next thing you know you're yelling at him or her. Then what? Do you start swinging your fists? Do you shove him backwards? Of course, you don't mean to really *hurt* him, but if there's no adult there, how far will things go?

No one is saying that you should *like* it if your sister is bugging you or if your brother grabs the seat you wanted to sit in. What matters is what you do about it. Taking the law into your own hands can seriously hurt someone. It's not easy, but it pays to keep your cool. That way—even if there are no adults around—you can work things out.

Control your words and your fists and you won't have to worry about accidentally injuring a family member or a friend.

devotion #85

NOT FAIR!

"Why do the wicked live on, growing old and increasing in power?"

—Job 21:7

The wicked probably live on because they take vitamin supplements and eat lots of yucky-tasting health food. Seriously though, this has always been a big question. It was a question in Job's day 3,500 years ago, and it's still a question today: if God blesses people who live righteous lives and judges those who do wrong, why do we see wicked men living to old age, getting richer, and having lots of toys to play with?

When you have to scrape your allowance together to buy a movie ticket, and you hear about some drug lord who lives in a mansion on some tropical island who has his own private movie theater and jet, it's easy to wonder, "Where's

God?" Did he leave the world on autopilot while he's off doing something else? It's even difficult to see a spoiled rich kid in your school who has it all while you don't have much. You wonder, "Doesn't God care?"

God does care and he's not way off somewhere out of cellular range. He does judge the wicked. He does bring the proud down. And he does reward the righteous. It just takes time. In the meantime, trust that God knows what's going on. Don't take the law into your own hands or try to even the score somehow. Let justice run its course. Give God space to take care of things.

God's on top of things and sees what's happening. Hang in there and he will reward you for doing what's right.

devotion #86

MUSCLES AND MORE

The glory of young men is their strength.

— Proverbs 20:29

God designed young men to be strong. You're not a man yet, but chances are you're already stronger than many girls your age. And the good news is, buddy, more muscles are on their way — lots of them! Usually when you're about twelve and a half, your body starts producing testosterone (tes-*toss*-ter-own), and that causes your bones to become thicker and stronger and your muscles to grow bigger — especially in your upper chest and shoulders.

To glory in the strength God gives you doesn't mean you're a glory hog. . .unless you're spending hours flexing your muscles in front of the mirror or putting up posters of yourself around town. We're not talking about that. We're talking about when you're just pumped about being what God made you to be — you're confident. Mom needs furniture moved. Who does she call? The kid with the muscles.

But don't just go for massive muscle mass and miss out on other good stuff. Don't just zero in on sports so that you end up a zero in the brains department. And be cool too — be a jock, but get along with others. Most important of all, be deeper — be real with God. Go for the whole package.

When God decided that men would be the protectors and warriors of the human race, he designed masculine muscles on his drawing board and thought the whole thing was cool. You should too. It's your glory.

Devotion #87

NOT LIMITED BY CIRCUMSTANCES

Jephthah the Gileadite was a mighty warrior. His father was Gilead; his mother was a prostitute.

— Judges 11:1

Jephthah was the son of Gilead and a prostitute. It must've been tough for Jephthah when he was growing up. His stepbrothers even kicked him out of the house because they didn't want to share their inheritance with him. On top of that, the city rulers told him to split. Jephthah went to Tob where he became a mighty warrior. Years later, when Ammonites began attacking his people, folks stopped trash-talking Jephthah's mom and started saying what a great guy Jephthah was.

Sometimes kids will talk down about other kids' parents. Maybe they

made dumb mistakes in the past. Or maybe your dad doesn't have a glamorous job or doesn't earn enough to take you to Disneyland. Perhaps your parents aren't as fun as other kids' parents. Or maybe it's just that as you get older, you start thinking it's cool to dis your parents.

Your parents may not be perfect, but you gotta respect them. Work with what you've got and go from there. You are where you are right now, but you don't have to be limited by your circumstances. Whatever your parents did or didn't do, it's up to *you* to make the most of your life. Where do *you* want to go?

God has a plan for your life, so pray and ask him to lead you into it. Then work hard to make it happen. And honor your parents in the meantime.

Devotion #88

BRING ON THE ANTS

Go to the ant, you sluggard; consider its ways and be wise! . . . How long will you lie there, you sluggard?

— Proverbs 6:6, 9

King Solomon wrote Proverbs, so he must've spent time studying ants. And since magnifying glasses hadn't been invented yet, you know he wasn't sitting there making them sizzle. Well, Solomon was on to something. Ants work hard. They may live in a dirt hill, but they keep it neat. Considering how *small* an ant's brain is, it must not take much thinking to keep things neat.

"How long will you lie there?" That *is* the question, isn't it? You gotta lie down sometimes; you need to veg. But exactly *how long* are you going to lie there? 'Cause, um, stuff needs to get done. Are your clothes an inch deep all over the floor like a second rug? Has your schoolbag disappeared somewhere in your room? Is there food all over your bedroom? Are their cookie crumbs on your sheets?

If you don't go to the ants to learn to clean up, the ants will come to *you*—guaranteed. They just love cookie crumbs and half-eaten food. Of course, once they come into your room, you gotta kill them. And what can you learn from a dead ant, right? Better to study the ants outside where they can be a great example to you.

Think about how hard that little ant works and how neat it keeps its digs. It'll make you wise.

devotion #89

WILLING BUT WEAK

"Watch and pray so that you will not fall into temptation. The spirit is willing, but the body is weak."
— Matthew 26:41

Jesus said these words in the garden of Gethsemane just before he was arrested, taken away, and crucified. When Jesus had warned Peter that this was coming, Peter had boasted that he was willing to go to prison and even die for Jesus. Peter's *spirit* was willing. He *wanted* to be all-out for Jesus. But when he was tested, he washed out. When the soldiers arrested Jesus, Peter took off running.

You've probably had moments like that. You want to do what's right, but sometimes you fail. Like if your mom can't figure out how to block a channel, you promise not to watch it. But then you get tempted and click to it anyway. And of course, your mom walks into the room right then, catches you like a deer in the headlights, and takes away your privileges.

You know what your weaknesses are, so avoid them. Like King Solomon said, "Do not set foot on the path of the wicked . . . Avoid it, do not travel on it; turn from it" (Proverbs 4:14–15). Don't even get near things that tempt you. If certain kids are always tempting you to do wrong stuff, stay away from them. If certain shows are off-limits, don't even *peek* at them.

Avoid temptation. And if you *can't* avoid it, pray for God's strength to resist it. He can give you the willpower to do what's right.

devotion #90

ALL FOR YOU

Then Pilate took Jesus and had him flogged. The soldiers twisted together a crown of thorns and put it on his head.

— John 19:1–2

After Pilate ordered Jesus to be flogged, the Roman soldiers beat Jesus with a cat-o'-nine-tails. This was a whip made of nine knotted cords. Jesus' back and legs and arms were cut wide open. If you've seen *The Passion of the Christ*, you know what we're talking about. Jesus lost so much blood it left him weak. As if that wasn't enough, the soldiers shoved a "crown" of sharp thorns down onto his head.

Ever gone into a thorn bush and slashed your legs? Ever sliced your finger or stepped on a nail? It can hurt so badly that it makes you scream.

Jesus knows what it's like to suffer terrible pain — stuff far worse than anything you've been through. His flesh was ripped open again and again.

Jesus suffered all this for you — even *before* he was crucified on the cross! Why did he do it? He didn't have to. He had a choice, and he could have avoided it. He suffered because he loved you. And *because* he loved you, he wanted to make you a child of God so that you could live in heaven forever. It doesn't get any better than that!

You can invite Jesus to come into your heart right now and make him Lord of your life. If you've already done that, then thank him that he's already given you eternal life.

Big Bad Bible Giants
Written by Ed Strauss
Softcover • ISBN 0-310-70869-9

Bible Angels and Demons
Written by Rick Osborne & Ed Strauss
Softcover • ISBN 0-310-70775-7

Bible Heroes & Bad Guys
Written by Rick Osborne,
Marnie Wooding & Ed Strauss
Softcover • ISBN 0-310-70322-0

Bible Wars & Weapons
Written by Rick Osborne,
Marnie Wooding & Ed Strauss
Softcover • ISBN 0-310-70323-9

Creepy Creatures & Bizarre Beasts from the Bible
Written by Rick Osborne & Ed Strauss
Softcover • ISBN 0-310-70654-8

Weird & Gross Bible Stuff
Written by Rick Osborne,
Quentin Guy & Ed Strauss
Softcover • ISBN 0-310-70484-7

COMING FALL 2007!

Bible Freaks & Geeks
Written by Ed Strauss
Softcover • ISBN 0-310-71309-9

Seriously Sick Bible Stuff
Written by Ed Strauss
Softcover • ISBN 0-310-71310-2

Available at your local bookstore!

zonder**kidz**

How to Draw Big Bad Bible Beasts

Written by Royden Lepp

Softcover • ISBN 0-310-71336-6

How to Draw Big Bad Bible Beasts depicts both familiar and unfamiliar creatures from Bible times. It will help young artists visualize scenes from the Bible and use their creativity to reproduce them.

How to Draw Good, Bad & Ugly Bible Guys

Written by Royden Lepp

Softcover • ISBN 0-310-71337-4

How to Draw Good, Bad & Ugly Bible Guys depicts the dress and armor of people from Bible times. It will help young artists visualize scenes from the Bible and use their creativity to reproduce them.

Available now at your local bookstore!

zonder**kidz**

Luke 2:52

Perfect for boys ages 8 to 12, the 2:52 series is based on Luke 2:52: "And Jesus grew in wisdom and stature, and in favor with God and men." Focusing on four primary areas of growth, this guiding verse can help boys become more like Jesus mentally (smarter), physically (stronger), spiritually (deeper), and socially (cooler). From Bibles and devotionals to fiction and nonfiction, with plenty of gross and gory mixed in, there is something for every boy.

Visit www.Luke252.com

noahge68

zonderkidz

We want to hear from you. Please send your comments about this book to us in care of zreview@zondervan.com. Thank you.

Grand Rapids, MI 49530
www.zonderkidz.com

ZONDERVAN.com/
AUTHORTRACKER
follow your favorite authors